Library of
Davidson College

Outstanding Dissertations in Music From British Universities

Edited by
John Caldwell
Oxford University

A Garland Series

Musical Analysis and the Listener

Nicholas Cook

Garland Publishing, Inc.
New York & London 1989

Copyright © 1989 by Nicholas Cook

Library of Congress Cataloging-in-Publication Data

Cook, Nicholas, 1950–
Music analysis and the listener / Nicholas Cook.
p. cm. — (Outstanding dissertations in music from British universities)
Thesis (Ph. D.)—University of Cambridge, 1982.
Bibliography: p.
ISBN 0-8240-0190-7 (alk. paper)
1. Musical analysis. 2. Music—Philosophy and aesthetics. I. Title. II. Series.
MT6.C775M9 1989
780'.1—dc19   89-1234

Designed by Valerie Mergentime

Printed on acid-free, 250-year-life paper.
Manufactured in the United States of America

Preface to the Garland Edition

Apart from the correction of some typographical errors and misspellings, what is contained in this volume is an unaltered reprint of the thesis I submitted to the University of Cambridge in 1982. This thesis was prompted by the discrepancy, as I saw it, between how musicians analyze music and how listeners experience it. My original intention was to develop new, phenomenologically-orientated techniques of analysis that would correspond more closely to listeners' perceptions of music than existing analytical procedures did. In other words I wanted to eliminate the discrepancy between analysis and experience. But eventually I came to the conclusion that this discrepancy is not only unavoidable but desirable, and even definitive of the analytical enterprise. The point of an analysis, I argued, is not to reduplicate the experience of a piece of music, but to modify it. When we experience music, we are not describing something that exists in an objective sense: we are developing new ways of imagining the music, new ways of representing or manipulating it, and so becoming better performers, composers or teachers. And it was this pragmatic conception of analysis that lay behind the *Guide to Musical Analysis* that I published a few years later.[1]

There are some points raised in this thesis that I have been able to refine or firm up since it was written. In particular I have carried out some experiments which reinforce the essentially speculative discussion of perceived tonal structure on pages 56–57 of the thesis.[2] I have also published the results of some informal tests of musical perception which were carried out as part of the research for the thesis but not described in it.[3] And a forthcoming book[4] further develops the theory of musical imagination that I originally put forward here, though its emphasis is on broader issues of aesthetics and culture rather than on the more immediate concerns of the musical analyst.

Nicholas Cook
Hong Kong, 1988

[1] London: J. M. Dent and New York: George Braziller (1987)

[2] 'The perception of large-scale tonal closure,' *Music Perception*, 5 (1987), 197–206.

[3] 'Musical form and the listener,' *Journal of Aesthetics and Art Criticism*, 46 (1987), 23-29.

[4] *Music, Imagination, and Culture*. London: Oxford University Press (in press).

Musical Analysis
and the Listener

Contents

Foreword — 3

Introduction — 4

1: Analysis and the varieties of musical listening — 24
'Functionalist' accounts of musical listening, p.24. The perception of form in music, p. 35. An elementary level of musical consciousness, p. 61. The varieties of musical listening, p. 69

2: Imagining Music — 81
The general properties of musical imagination, p. 81. The musician's imagery of sound, p. 87. Composition and prediction, p. 100. Imagination as a stylistic and historical factor, p. 116

3: Musical and psychological explanation — 124
Introductory, p. 124. Theories of unconscious psychological functioning implicit in modern analysis, p. 129. The score as a basis for analytical deduction, p. 143

4: A rationale of analytical practice — 163
Analytical argument and its value, p. 163. Analytical image and analytical listening, p. 175. Criteria of analytical adequacy, p. 186. Analysis and contemporary musical culture, p. 196

Summary — 204

List of sources cited — 211

Foreword

The subject matter of this thesis does not wholly fall within the confines of musical analysis proper, but from time to time spills over into such adjacent areas as aesthetics, phenomenology and psychology. It is however not intended as a contribution to any of these neighbouring disciplines, but is written from the viewpoint of the musical analyst and with the intention that any such material should have some fairly direct application to musical analysis. Although it concludes by setting out a rationale of analytical practice, and also incorporates a sustained critique of rigorously deductive methods of analysis, much of this thesis is taken up not so much with argument as with detailed description. I hope that the descriptive accounts offered of musical listening and of musical imagination will not only be of an intrinsic interest, but will also act as a counterbalance to some of the rather premature theorization - often of an extremely complex nature - that is often found in contemporary musical analysis.

In view of this proliferation of detail and in the interests of clarity, I have set out some of the principal issues discursively in an Introduction; in addition there is at the end a chapter-by-chapter summary of the argument which is intended to be read in conjunction with the main text. The bibliography however is restricted to such works as are referred to, in an abbreviated form, in the text and notes.

I am required to state that this thesis is the result of my own work and incorporates no research carried out in collaboration with others. However I wish to acknowledge, with thanks, the many ways in which I have been helped by my supervisor, Professor Alexander Goehr.

Cambridge, August 1982

Introduction

I

There is a curious ambivalence in the image music has with the general public. On the one hand, it is thought of as a universal language, an art that speaks directly to the emotions and is therefore accessible to almost everybody. On the other hand, it is thought of as forbiddingly technical and 'difficult', as if it required great learning to understand music properly. The same ambivalence can be seen in popular ideas about the act of musical composition. On the one hand this is seen as the spontaneous effusion of inspired genius; on the other as an abstruse and cerebral calculation – this latter charge, of course, being levelled principally against twentieth century composers. As long ago as 1946 Schoenberg attempted to show that this supposed discrepancy between heart and brain, as he put it, was based on a fallacy: "It is not the heart alone which creates all that is beautiful, emotional, pathetic, affectionate, and charming; nor is it the brain alone which is able to produce the well-constructed, the soundly-organized, the logical, and the complicated. First, everything of supreme value in art must show heart as well as brain. Second, the real creative genius has no difficulty in controlling his feelings mentally; nor must the brain produce only the dry and unappealing while concentrating on correctness and logic". Thus he concluded that in music "sentimentality has its origin in a very poor heart".[1]

Nevertheless the relationship between heart and brain in music has continued to be problematical. Nowhere has this been more evident than in the highly technical varieties of compositional and analytical thinking that have developed since the end of the Second World War, both in Europe and America: the complexity of abstract thought found in articles in <u>Die Reihe</u> and <u>Perspectives of New Music</u>, as well as in compositions themselves, is a potent symbol of the enduring gap between culturally legitimate and commercially viable music. Nor is the problem here merely one of audiences reached. It is also a question of the relationship between such highly cerebral compositional or analytical categories, and the listener's aural, and emotional, experience of the music. Even in the case of those popularizing analyses intended to reach a wider audience, such as the series Antony Hopkins broadcasts under the title 'Talking about Music', the relationship between technical exposition and ordinary aesthetic response can seem strained. There is, for example, an unspoken aesthetic in such programmes which lays great stress on the unity of musical form, the tightness of relationship between such form and every detail of the music, and the authenticity of the compositional process as the clarification of a basic emotion or idea; indeed this aesthetic is to some extent built into the normal vocabulary of musical analyses, into terms such as underlying tonality, structural downbeat, and prolongation. Now it can be argued that any vocabulary for musical description must impose aesthetic and other frames of reference upon the music. The ethnomusicologist Charles Seeger[2] has emphasized the inevitable discrepancy between verbal and musical structures; he has shown the cultural assumptions and values that are built even into our conventional notation, which thus creates distinctions where non-Western musics do not intend them and overlooks those that are intended. And the phenomenological investigations of, for instance, F. Joseph Smith[3] confirm the extent to which our whole thinking about music is determined by verbal and visual models which have no direct relationship to the immediately aural experiencing of music. No words or graphs can therefore be a perfect analogue of the listener's experience.

Nevertheless the particular discrepancies between aural experience and analytical description cannot be wholly accounted for in such general terms. Specific and substantial discrepancies remain. For example our analytical emphasis on large-scale tonal unity, and its aesthetic importance in defining musical form, is predicated on the listener's ability to perceive the tonic on which a piece opens as identical to that on which it ends. But people who have listened to good music for years and with pleasure, but who have never had even the most rudimentary musical education, do not know what a tonic is. It is not simply that they know the thing but not the word for it. It takes some time to teach such a person exactly what is meant by a tonic, that is to say what he is meant to be listening out for and (so to speak) withdrawing from the sound; he has, in fact, to learn to perceive the sound in a new way, rather than simply learning to name what he has always perceived. (Musicians tend to forget the amount of learning that goes into these rudimentary discriminations, because they acquire it as a byproduct of the early stages of instrumental tuition.) And even when our untutored listener has learned what a tonic is, it is by no means clear that he will find it easy or even possible to perceive the identity of two tonics that are separated by five or ten minutes of music. But in that case what is it that we are talking about when we speak of large-scale tonal unity, if not of perceptual judgements actually made by listeners?

There are two ways in which a rational solution may be found for this dilemma and which therefore serve to justify musical analysis carried out in such terms. The first possibility is simply to accept that listening to music is difficult, and that ordinary listeners do in fact often fail to comprehend music properly. Consequently the analyst's function is to explain to the layman what he should listen out for, so that he will thereafter understand the music better. Such explanation can be done in terms of compositional or historical categories, or alternatively by means of categories specially designed to represent the aesthetically important properties of musical sound in a non-technical manner - for example by means of graphs representing degree of regularity in the musical movement, perceived density of sound and so forth. These are the mainstay of music appreciation as it is taught in American liberal arts colleges and elsewhere. No doubt the appreciation movement has had many benefits in bringing fine music to the attention of people who might otherwise never have encountered it. At the same time there is underlying it a distinctly elitist and indeed patronizing conception of music. It seems to be based on the assumption that the layman's experience of music is merely an impoverished version of the more technical perception of which a musically-trained person is capable. It deals more or less entirely with isolated masterpieces of music, which are presented rather like precious objects that have survived from a remote past and whose appreciation therefore requires a special skill - rather like that acquired by the connoisseur of Italian Quattrocento painting. Now to the extent that the music appreciation movement is elitist in its interests and methods, it narrows its range of purview and ignores important characteristics of music. Much pleasure is derived from musical works that are not masterpieces. More important - and indeed this is perhaps the single most striking characteristic of music - most people will enjoy music about whose technical and formal structure they know nothing; special training is rarely of more than tangential importance for those who simply wish to derive aesthetic pleasure from listening to music (as opposed to being able to read, perform or compose it, all of which require training of some sort). To accept musical analysis as showing not how music is heard but how it should be is, therefore, to ignore most of the enjoyment that people do, in fact, derive from music; and it is this more ordinary enjoyment, as much as that of the connoisseur, that this thesis is concerned with.

The second possibility I referred to is more complex. This is to maintain that analysis has to do with what people do hear rather than what they should, but that the actual topic of analysis is not the musical experience itself. Rather analysis is about some kind of substrate that underlies the experience. And the specific properties of this substrate need not necessarily coincide with what the listener consciously perceives as such - just as, for example, the physical properties of a pointillist painting do not coincide with the shimmering effect it makes upon the viewer (unless the viewer comes too close, in which case he will see the separate spots of colour but at the expense of the overall effect). In the same way, the argument would go, analysis has to do with what underlies the listener's experience, but there is no reason to demand an immediate correlate in his conscious experience to every analytical statement. Hence the apparent discrepancy between the two.

In assessing this possibility the first step is to determine what sort of thing this substrate might be, and here the difficulties begin. The simplest answer would be: the score. And it is true that most analysis of music is, in the first instance, analysis of the score. But it is rarely just analysis of the score; instead the score is used as a convenient basis for making statements about the music, and such aspects of the score as have no relationship to the sound are for the most part ignored – not only such obvious irrelevancies as the colour or size of the score, but things like the curious enharmonic intervals found in harp writing, for example, or the barlines that vary as between original and revised editions of Stravinsky. Such notational distinctions may have consequences for performance, but they have no direct correlate either in the physical sound of the music – the movement of air in the auditorium – or in the listener's perception of that sound. So the substrate of experience that the analyst talks about can hardly be identified literally with either the score or the performers' actions; at most, it can be seen as coinciding with these to the extent that they have consequences for the aesthetic experience of the music. On the other hand what the analyst says cannot be reduced to assertions about the physical characteristics of sound, as might have been maintained by nineteenth-century acousticians. Obviously there is in sound a physical substrate to the listener's experience, but the difficulty lies in making a connection between this and what the analyst is talking about. As is well known, there is no direct correlation between the physicist's categories of frequency, amplitude and spectral complexity and the music analyst's categories of pitch, dynamics and tone quality; each of these categories proves upon investigation to be dependent on the others, as well as on such purely psychological factors as the listener's degree of wakefulness. Hence we experience as musically satisying what J.B. Davies calls "an array of sounds which, according to scientific evidence, should be cacophonous to a high degree". He continues: "the basic building blocks of music thus consist not of simple physical events, but of people's responses to those events".[4] The substrate to musical experience which musical analysis is concerned with must, therefore, be seen in terms of response categories - that is to say, categories which may be embodied in sound but which are functionally distinct from the sound itself. And indeed this distinction between sound and musical function, and hence between an immediate sensory registration and a genuinely musical response to sound, is fundamental to twentieth century analysis. As Leonard B. Meyer puts it, "music is directed not <u>to</u> the senses, but <u>through</u> the senses and to <u>the mind</u>".[5] The distinction is however more often made implicitly, in the course of a musical description, than in such explicitly psychological terms. For example, writing on heterophony Kurt Sachs observed how in primitive music "the players, like the listeners, accept that they are playing in unison; they overlook the consonances and dissonances that occur, and tolerate as unimportant careless entries, ragged endings and inexact lengthenings and shortening of individual notes". The assumption here is that the aesthetic meaning of the music derives from the musical structures as they might be classified by the analyst (unison, octaves, regular rhythmic relationships and so forth), as distinct from the sonic concretion in which these structures are embodied; so that Sachs could write of public singing in churches (with its characteristic rhythmic drag) that "such anarchistic singing would be intolerable if its purpose, and the attention of those present, were directed towards artistically satisfying results".[6]

Given such a distinction between physical sound on the one hand, and the aesthetically significant categories on which musical structures are based on the other, questions still remain: just what does the significance of these categories derive from, and therefore what exact relationship do they bear to musical style? A number of answers to these questions is possible. The simplest is that meaningful categories of musical structure (such as the triad) derive directly from laws of nature, as has been maintained by orthodox Schenkerians: thus music has aesthetic meaning because it embodies these laws. Alternatively, the functional categories of any given musical style may be seen as determined by cultural conventions, whether explicitly codified or not: music has aesthetic effect either because it conforms to these conventional norms (this is supposed by theorists who see music as functioning analogously to language) or, in contrast, because it deviates from them (as proposed, for example, by Meyer or by Max Weber's account of the musical virtuoso[7]). But in all these cases musical analysis is seen as the same kind of enterprise, namely as the discovery (and hence the application in particular instances) of the categories that actually function in the aesthetic perception of music, and of the principles that govern the association of such categories into musical structures. And equally, in all these cases, musical listeners themselves may be quite unaware of such categories and principles of formation. Thus Kolinski, who believes that musical structures derive from natural laws, argues that the emphasis nowadays placed by most ethnomusicologists on folk awareness of structural principles is unjustified, on the grounds that "a stone has not to be aware of the law of gravity in order to drop".[8] Again, where it is suggested that it is conventional norms that matter, the analogy with language shows how it is possible for people to respond correctly to structures based on complex formal principles of which they have only the haziest explicit knowledge.

Here, then, we would appear to have a resolution to the discrepancy of analytical account and listener's experience: when we analyze music we are not talking directly about the experience, but an underlying level at which musical sound is perceived as being aesthetically meaningful. And it makes no difference from the point of view of the music's functioning, and hence of the validity of its analysis, whether these perceptual judgements are conscious (so that an analytical category or connection will be immediately experienced) or not. Either way a psychological assertion is involved: the music functions thus because that is how it is perceived. Either the categories and principles of musical functioning are intrinsically psychological; or else if they are not (for instance, if they can be reduced to a strictly logical formulation) then they must still have psychological consequences for perception. In fact this whole rationale of musical analysis in its many varieties can be seen as an expression of Schoenberg's maxim that "every musical explanation must be at the same time psychological";[9] and this holds whether the analysis is explicitly couched in psychological terms, or (as more often) is only psychological by implication. Furthermore the aims of twentieth-century analysis are, by and large, psychological in that the experienced properties of musical compositions - their emotional impact, aesthetic value and so on - are explained in terms of the properties of the stimulus and the principles governing its interpretation by the listener. Meyer for instance makes this clear: "once the norms of a style have been ascertained [he writes], the study and analysis of the affective content of a particular work in that style can be made without continual and explicit reference to the responses of the listener or critic. That is, subjective content can be discussed objectively".[10] The aim is therefore to bypass the listener's subjective judgement and set up a theory of musical meaning in its place. Meyer's account is, of course, explicitly psychological, as well as musicological, in its reduction of experienced emotion to formal psychological and musical structures. But aesthetic valuation is just as much a component of the listener's experience as emotion, so that the same applies to any attempt to explain musical value in terms of formal structures discovered through musical analysis. And there can be few analyses that do not assume the possibility of some such correlation, even if the assumption lies in no more than the fact that the piece was thought worthy of analysis in the first place.

II

In this thesis I argue that the categories normally employed by musical analysts bear little relationship to the psychological structures or processes of musical perception. It is of course difficult, if not impossible, to discover what these structures or processes might be by immediate observation; instead they have to be deduced from such behaviour as is directly observable, such as playing an instrument. Now the fine control of instrumental performance - especially on instruments whose intonation is not fixed in advance, such as the violin - involves aural perception on the performer's part; good intonation, in a solo context at least, demands that the violinist hear himself play. Hence his performance can reasonably be regarded as "an outstanding indicator of the real activity of the nervous system ... whose output is well correlated with the neural mechanisms involved in tonal perception";[11] that is to say, as corresponding more or less directly to the psychological determination of musical structures at this level. It also seems reasonable to assume that such determinants apply not only to the perception of intervals in violin music, but also in the case of instruments where intonation is fixed and where these fine values of intonation must therefore be wholly psychological. Qualifications will no doubt be necessary as to how direct this correspondence between perception and performance may be if a properly psychological theory of musical intonation is to be developed; but for purposes of assessing the significance of the music analyst's categories it is sufficient that precise intonation varies according to the musical context and that these variations do not correspond to any analytical categorizations of musical intervals. Nor are such variations simply a matter of chance or indifference, because such evidence as is available shows the correspondence of intonation and musical context to be fairly consistent, and an important determinant of the perceived quality of performance. Good intonation is after all one of the principal criteria of good violin playing, but one which can only be assessed by ear. The judgement of whether the intonation of a given note is 'right' or 'wrong', whether made by performer or listener, is unmediated by critical reflection; it is simply a matter of what sounds right in the particular context, in the same way as deciding where on the wall a picture should hang is a matter of an immediate judgement of what looks right.[12] And the decision involved cannot be explained by the musical analyst's terminology for intervals - whether equal-tempered or enharmonic - because the performer's and listener's determinations are considerably more fine-grained, and more sensitive to musical context, than the analyst's. Thus the intervallic categories built into musical notation are not so much wrong; rather they are loose, denoting an approximate value only.[13] They acquire a precise denotation, such as musical performance demands, only by virtue of the performer's aural judgement, and if it is to be correct this judgement requires of the performer that he listen not only to himself but to his fellow performers too. Most musicians will recognize the experience of playing with someone who plays his part stiffly and correctly, without adjusting his intonation, pacing or dynamics to other people's. It is like trying to hold a conversation with someone who will not listen but simply says his piece.

Musical performance is therefore not a formal situation in the way that a game is. Games are defined by precisely codified rules that can be stated in advance; indeed learning the rules is a necessary first step in learning how to play the game, and to this extent it is possible to grasp the working of a game 'in theory'. By contrast, it is very difficult to understand what music is about 'in theory'. It is like Alice's game, or rather non-game, of croquet: the precise meaning of the rules changes from one context to another, and the rigid and inflexible notions that non-musicians tend to have about how music works arise from the failure to appreciate this. Only exceptionally does music evolve a style so narrowly defined and so highly codified that it becomes possible to reduce its working wholly to predetermined rules; that is to say, that it becomes possible to predict with certainty what will sound right and what will sound wrong purely on the basis of a formal calculation. 'Bach style', which is more or less a pedagogical invention, is one such exception, although even here some degree of musical taste and imagination is probably necessary to produce tolerable results, as well as conformity to explicit rules. Normally however the fit between codified rule and experienced effect is not so good. More often therefore writing music is a much more fragmentary process, in which such formal calculation as there may be alternates with trying passages out on the piano to see if they sound right or not; there is a kind of counterpoint between structural intention and aural effect, such that the final product is unlikely to be exactly what was originally anticipated - especially where the details of the music are concerned. Nor, when the work is finished, will it be possible to explain or deduce everything that sounds right (or wrong) from the notational categories in which the music is, so to speak, kept between performances. Only at a fairly large, and crude, scale of compositional organization will the aesthetically important formations (that is to say, the things that will be judged 'right' or 'wrong') be visible in the score; the symmetrical balance between the various formal parts of Tchaikowsky's <u>Francesca da Rimini</u>, for instance, is easy to see in the score, and refers to a level at which the judgement of 'rightness' involved is probably not specifically aural at all - thus it is essentially no different from the disposition of an architectural facade. But the aesthetic working of the details frequently cannot be deduced from the score in such a manner. Instead the score has to be read as music - whether in actual performance, or simply through attempting to imagine the effect the music will make. And now we have ceased to treat the music as an objective structure defined in terms of the intervallic categories of notation; our analysis no longer deals with formal relations embodied in sound, but rather with experienced sound relations. We are 'hearing' the intervals shown in the score in terms of the precise values they will take on in the particular musical context. We are making sense of the musical details, in short, precisely to the extent that we are treating the notated intervals as a rough and informal approximation to the intended sound; and the same may well apply to the rhythmic, and certainly to the dynamic, indications in the score. But if, instead of reading the score in this sense, we make a detailed deductive analysis of it, then we are attempting to base precise formal deductions of aesthetic significance on categories which are themselves imprecise and informal. We run two risks in so doing: first of missing aesthetically important discriminations of which the score shows nothing, and second of imputing to the experience itself properties which merely belong to its external representation in the score.

If these criticisms are valid, then they are not without consequences for the sense in which the analyst can be legitimately thought of as explaining music. The formalist view - that is to say, the view according to which structures of musical significance are logically distinct from musical sound - has been put quite explicitly by Babbitt. "There is", he says, "but one kind of language, one kind of method for the verbal formulation of 'concepts' and the verbal analysis of such formulations: 'scientific' language and 'scientific' method... Statements about music must conform to those verbal and methodological requirements which attend the possibility of meaningful discourse in any domain".[14] By this he means that it must be possible to give a precise definition of the various terms of a theoretical language, such that its formulations are unambiguous and its predictions empirically testable. As we have seen, however, the intervallic categories employed by analysts - including Boretz himself - are only capable of such explicit formulation at an abstract level; that is, a level at which they refer not to what musicians do but to what they represent themselves as doing. In other words these categories are without a direct psychological foundation either in musical performance or, as far as one can tell, in ordinary aesthetic perception. Whereas the formal analyst assumes that the function of musical sound is to communicate precise structural categories, the truth would appear to be more nearly the reverse: that is to say, the function of notational categories is to communicate sonorous values whose precise determination is a matter of purely aural judgement. Consequently a scientific theory of music, if it is to conform to Babbitt's methodological criteria, would involve discarding the convenient and conventional notation of musical intervals (and no doubt those of rhythms, dynamics and so on) and adopting in their place a much more direct and detailed representation of musical sound. At the theoretical level, that is to say in terms of the general connections between psychological determinants and musical style, this may well be a very interesting, if difficult, line of research. It is however hard to imagine that such a microscopic involvement in musical sound would ever allow of an ascent to the larger scale of musical form, as it occurs in specific compositions, in which the analyst is primarily interested. In other words the kind of scientific enterprise that would fulfil Babbitt's demands might be worth while but it would hardly be musical analysis in the sense in which we normally intend the term. In fact whereas Babbitt regards unambiguous objectivity as the only sense in which an analysis can have meaning, it is really by no means obvious that this is an appropriate aim for the musical analyst. This is perhaps best shown by comparing the sort of analysis that musicians do with various other types of analysis that can have music as their object.

Music can be studied from the viewpoints of anthropology, psychology, phenomenology and aesthetics - others could no doubt be mentioned but these are the main ones. In each case deductive generalizations are made from individual instances, and all these disciplines aim at some kind of certainty (though in very different ways). At the same time, the conclusions of all these disciplines are at best tangential to 'musical analysis' in the sense in which musicians use that term. For example, phenomenologists, aestheticians and aesthetically-minded music theorists all agree that the experience of music is largely determined by synaesthetic associations. In particular Collingwood, Coker, Hornbostel, Kurth and Zuckerkandl - among many others - emphasize the role kinaesthetic imagery plays in musical listening. Again, anthropologists and anthropologically-minded music theorists emphasize the role social factors play in determining the response to music; as John Blacking puts it, "unless the formal analysis begins as an analysis of the social situation that generates the music, it is meaningless".[15] If all this is true, then, the musical sound is only one term in a complex equation; the significance of the formal structures found in it, together with the principles that govern them, will only emerge when all the other factors are taken into acount. To attempt to analyze musical sound in isolation would be like trying to analyze a novel from its appearance on the printed page, ignoring all the narrative, emotional and plain English meaning that it conveys.

Considered in its own terms an argument like this is probably irrefutable; music is not analyzable as we analyze it, if by analysis is meant a scientifically legitimate investigation which has unambiguously verifiable conclusions as its aim. But to say this is only to underline the extent to which analysis, as practised by music analysts, is something other than a scientific enterprise; neither its methods, nor the criteria of adequacy by which a musical analysis asks to be judged, are scientific. Thus musical analysts constantly employ a terminology which, as theorists like Boretz have demonstrated, is incapable of any precise interpretation; they use terms like 'melody', 'cadence' and 'suprising' which are so loosely defined in terms of formal structure as to be more or less meaningless as a basis for theoretical generalization. Boretz dismisses such analysis as merely "persuasive".[16] He is right: the analyst does indeed marshal arguments which are intended to persuade his reader to 'hear' a given piece in a particular way; it is his reader's belief as regards the specific music in question, rather than certainty at a theoretical level, at which the analyst aims. Boretz' critique may well be justified in the case of those secondary literatures that a few well-established analytical methods have produced; there is for example a considerable Schenkerian corpus which consists of argument at a purely theoretical level rather than in terms of concrete applications, and here it is difficult to see quite what criteria of validity could be invoked if not scientific. On the whole, however, Boretz' argument - and with it the whole trend towards making musical analysis into an exact science - misses the point, not because its logic is deficient but because such logic is not appropriate to the circumstances.

At the beginning of his <u>Harmonielehre</u>, Schoenberg wrote that "one would have to go back to the subject, to the sense of hearing, if one would establish a real theory of tones.

Now it is not my aim to present such a theory or even a theory of harmony, nor do I possess enough ability and knowledge to do so; I am rather simply trying to present the harmonic means of music in such a way that they can be directly applied in practice. It could happen, nevertheless, that in this way I achieve more than I am actually striving for, since my goal is just clarity and comprehensiveness of presentation. But however little that would displease me, it is still not my purpose. Therefore, whenever I theorize, it is less important whether these theories be right than whether they be useful as comparisons to clarify the object and to give the study perspective".[17] Like others of Schoenberg's disclaimers, this should probably not be taken too literally as a statement of his ambitions. There is a great deal of theorizing in <u>Harmonielehre</u>, and it ends with a query as to what the psychological laws may be that govern the composition of complex chords and tone-colour; laws, that is, which would hold for all music, rather than merely expressing a particular aesthetic value. And the aim of making deductions concerning music on the basis of established psychological principles is more evident still in those who have been influenced by Schoenberg's thinking – in the explicit psychology of Ehrenzweig and Keller, for example, or the reconstructions of the historical processes of harmonic evolution offered by Lissa, Abraham and Samson. In all these applications the aim would appear to be some kind of general truth rather than simply usefulness within a given cultural context. Nevertheless the distinction Schoenberg makes seems to me an essential one for the musical analyst. Indeed if musical analysis can be regarded as a legitimate branch of learning, this is not because it is a kind of undercover science, explaining musical phenomena once and for all, and from a detached and objective viewpoint. It is because it explains music from within; that is to say, because it is part of our musical culture.

Notes

1: Style and Idea, p. 75-6.

2: Studies in Musicology 1935-75, Chapters 1, 8.

3: Experiencing Musical Sound, Chapter 2.

4: The Psychology of Music, p. 42-7. More detailed correlations of physical and psychological parameters will be found in Ward, Musical Perception.

5: Music, the Arts and Ideas, p. 271.

6: These quotations (from Sachs' article Heterophonie in Die Musick in Geschichte und Gegenwart) are translated on the sleeve of Kagel's Heterophonie (DGG records).

7: Rational and Social Foundations of Music, p. xxxix.

8: The Structure of Music: Diversification versus Constraint, p. 11

9: Theory of Harmony, p. 164.

10: Emotion and Meaning in Music, p. 32.

11: Boomsliter and Creel, Research Potentials in Auditory Characteristics of Violin Tone, p. 1989.

12: Cf. Scruton, Aesthetics of Architecture, p. 201.

13: Against this it could be argued that the 'theoretical' values of intervals - whther equal-tempered, Pythagorean or whatever - do constitute psychologically real norms but that performance intonation also embodies "artistic deviations from the exact or rigid" (Seashore, Psychology of Music, p. 249). This argument is difficult to refute, because it would be compatible with almost any data whatever. In any case what this suggestion is really saying is that the precise value of such deviations – which varies with musical context – is aesthetically decisive, in which case notational categories of interval (which do not vary in the same way) would still be at best an incomplete statement of the psychological functions fufilled by intervals. So this suggestion makes little difference in practice.

14: Past and Present Concepts of the Nature and Limits of Music, p. 3.

15: How Musical is Man?, p. 71.

16: Metavariations, PNM Fall/Winter 1969, p. 13.

17: Theory of Harmony, p. 18-9.

Chapter One:

Analysis and the varieties of musical listening

'Functionalist' accounts of musical listening

In the twentieth century it has become normal to describe pieces of music by means of a much more technical vocabulary than was formerly the case. Ever since the Greeks, it is true, there has been a specialized, theoretical terminology for music; but it was used to set out the general principles of correct style, rather then to elucidate the qualities of particular compositions. Thus Thomas Morley's <u>Plain and Easy Introduction to Practical Music</u> or Rameau's theoretical writings are both technical enough, but neither can be considered analytical because neither is concerned with particular pieces of music. A distinction was implicitly made between the purely technical matter of style – that is to say, a musical language which might be well-formed or badly-formed – and the particular expressive content of a given piece. When individual pieces were described, this was done basically in terms of their effects upon the listener – as in the baroque doctrine of the affects, or in the literary evocations of music current particularly in the nineteenth century (for example, in his book on gypsy music Liszt described how its rhythms, "taking us unawares, are forcibly remindful of the capricious bounds of fawn and deer when startled"[1]).

One of the principal strands in modern music, no doubt deriving largely from Hanslick's championing of Brahms, has been a belief that it is improper to make such a distinction between technical means and expressive effect in music. Most of Schoenberg's innovations from the First Chamber Symphony on can be seen as attempts to reinstate the aesthetic significance of formal structure in music, in reaction to the rather amorphous sensualism typified by Richard Strauss; even in works like <u>Pierrot Lunaire</u> and the <u>Five Orchestral Pieces</u>, which the listener experiences almost entirely in coloristic or expressive terms, the most elaborately detailed contrapuntal devices show Schoenberg's concern with the formal properties of the musical object. Again, such miniature compositions as the last of the <u>Six Little Piano Pieces</u> Op. 19 can be divided into patterns of antecedent, consequent, developmental transition and abbreviated restatement (bars 1, 5, 7 and 9 respectively). It is true that Schoenberg did not see these formal properties as being of an intrinsic aesthetic significance. "Order [he wrote] is not demanded by the object, but by the subject... The adaptation of what the artist really wants to present, its reduction to fit the boundaries of form, of artistic form, is necessary only because of our inability to grasp the undefined and unordered. The order we call artistic form is not an end in itself, but an expedient".[2] But this is only to underline his belief that the aesthetic justification for formal structure is that it fulfilled some function within the experience of the music as a unified whole; thus the principal aesthetic intention behind the type of motivic analysis Schoenberg practised was to show how everything in a fine composition could be derived from some underlying musical idea or shape. Similarly Schenker, in his analyses, aimed to distinguish the musically essential from the gratuitous by showing how everything could be derived from a fundamental structure; and the aesthetic and even normative tone is at least as strong in Schenker as it is in Schoenberg. In this way both their analytical methods developed from a vigorous belief in certain aesthetic values

- values which were influential in other contemporary arts too. In architecture for example all ornamentation which fulfilled, or expressed, no structural function was swept away; and in adopting the same slogan as the architects - 'functionalism'[3] - musical analysts of the inter-war period identified aesthetic value in music with the coherence and unity of its formal structure. Analytical emphasis was thus placed firmly on the musical composition as a kind of artefact or object.

Since most current analysis derives more or less directly from either Schoenberg or Schenker, it has become the norm for analysts to think of the experience of music in this 'functionalist' manner, that is to say in terms of the objective elements or structures that are perceived; rather than (as in the nineteenth century) primarily in terms of the overall effect the music has upon the listener. In consequence the process of musical listening has tended to be seen as a form of higher-level mental activity in which the compositional structure is in some sense reconstituted by the listener. The origins of this view of musical listening in a particular early twentieth-century aesthetic stance have been so far disregarded that this is commonly cited by aestheticians as a precondition for any properly musical listening. According to Stuart Hampshire, for instance, "there is a recognized distinction between art and mere entertainment ... Music is understood as art if, and only if, the listener is intellectually active in listening to it. If he remains intellectually passive and attends only to the surface play of sound, he is treating the music only as entertainment ... The listener creates the impression in his own mind by tracing the structure of the work for himself, using his own natural imagery and his musical memory. If no parallel working of the listener's mind is interesting, the work has failed as art".[4] The main factual (as opposed to normative) assertion of this is that listening to music involves some kind of internal representation of the music that mediates between the sound that is perceived at any given moment and the aesthetically comprehended structure of the whole. Schoenberg refers to such internal representation over and over again in his writings: "one can comprehend only what one can keep in mind", for example, or "if ... in music a figure is so constituted ... that I cannot recognize it and remember it, than correct understanding of all that follows ... is impossible".[5] Indeed according to Roger Sessions the role of memory in aesthetic perception is so crucial that "the accurate memory of sounds heard coincides with the understanding of them".[6] On the other hand, Meyer argues that memory alone is an insufficient criterion for aesthetic response: "neither memorization nor performance necessarily entail understanding ... It is possible to read, memorize and perform music that one does not really understand".[7] Clearly therefore he sees the aesthetic response to music - "really understanding the music", as he puts it - as a specifically mental function.

While their details may vary, then, all these accounts of musical listening adopt a specific aesthetic stance in that they seek to distinguish a correct understanding of music from a simple sensory registration of it, one of the criteria for this being in each case some kind of adequate internal representation of the musical structure. Another such criterion has to do with the nature of the perceived relations.

Schoenberg defined tonality as "the art of combining tones in such successions and such harmonies or successions of harmonies, that the relation of all events to a fundamental tone is made possible".[8] In accordance with this, his <u>Structural Functions of Harmony</u> is essentially an attack upon the conventional terminology of modulation, according to which pieces go from one key through a succession of others in a more or less anecdotal manner. Rather, Schoenberg argued, "there is only <u>one tonality</u> in a piece, and every segment formerly considered as another tonality is only a region, or harmonic contrast within that tonality".[9] He even drew up "charts of the Regions" which represent by graphic means the precise relationship of each key to the tonic. The implication is that to respond aesthetically to a sequence of keys - to understand it as music - involves the perception of each key as specifically related in terms of this overall transformational structure: Schoenberg is scathing about performances that render impossible such a unified perception of key relationships - "listening to a concert [he wrote], I often find myself unexpectedly 'in a foreign country', not knowing how I got there; a modulation has occurred which escaped my comprehension".[10] Schenkerian analysis is equally concerned with explaining the aesthetic effect of a particular musical configuration in terms of its precise role within the overall, unitary structure of a given piece; the series of graphs which constitutes a Schenker analysis can be seen as showing the transformational relationships between the two, and though the properties of such transformations were not rigorously defined by Schenker there have been a number of attempts in the last twenty years to state them in a more rigorous, and sometimes axiomatic form.[11] The American composers and analysts attempting this have been particularly fond of stressing the analogy between the way in which Schenker-based analysis explained the musical surface in terms of its underlying, unitary structure and the way in which contemporary linguists derive particular utterances from underlying grammatical prototypes. This, they seem to have felt, showed the basis of such explanations in general psychological principles, imparting to their analyses something of the the objective character of linguistic research.[12] It also imparted to their analyses, and indeed to their compositions, that aesthetic predisposition towards extreme structural complexity which is the logical consequence of Schoenberg's and Schenker's approach to music.

Explaining the aesthetic experience of music in this way, that is to say as a rationally mediated response to the complex but coherent structural relationships inherent in the musical object, involves making assertions about musical listening on one or both of two different levels, which we might call the internal and the external (and both of which are mirrored in the formal study of language). By the 'internal' level I refer to the hidden psychological processes that go on when someone listens: as in the perception of speech, so in music the listener might be unconscious of the perceptual unravelling of the stimulus structures that determine his experience, so that the precise nature of such processes would be discoverable only through experiment or deduction rather than through introspection. For example, Schoenberg's account of tonal relations would not necessarily imply that the listener should be able to specify the relation to the tonic of each region through which the music passes; his perception of these tonal relationships might be purely unconscious.

Nevertheless, if such unconscious processes could be discovered and related to the structural properties of the musical stimulus, they would constitute an objective explanation of what the listener does consciously experience – in this case, the unity of the work as a tonal argument. In this way one of the senses in which a particular musical configuration can be seen as fulfilling, or not fulfilling, a structural function is in terms of hidden psychological processes; and accordingly 'functional' analysis is, or at least can be, by implication a theory of unconscious perception. Such implications are very far-reaching and discussion of them is therefore postponed until Chapter Threee.

The 'external' aspect, which is what this chapter is about, concerns what is consciously communicated in the chain of composition, performance and listening; that is to say, those properties of musical experience which can be discovered by introspection, or by a careful description of a particular experience. 'Function' can here be defined more or less wholly in terms of compositional intentions. Does the musical surface serve to articulate the intended formal structure clearly? Are the intended relationships between the various musical materials sufficiently clear? Such questions are posed by the very language of conventional analysis ('exposition', 'recapitulation' and so forth), and they imply a particular compositional attitude towards the musical listener. For example, few composers have ever been as concerned for the listener as Schoenberg. In <u>Style and Idea</u> he described the steps he took while composing the First Chamber Symphony in order to ensure that the pace of musical development should not outstrip the capacity of an "average good listener" (as he put it[13]) to follow the music. In other words he seems to have begun with certain structural intentions, and the detailed compositional process was concerned with their successful communication: indeed his worries have clearly left a mark upon the music. For example, the principal second subject (rehearsal number 21) sounds almost like a caricature of what second subjects were expected to sound like in those days; and those very prominent repeated chords between numbers 27 and 32 were no doubt intended to underline a structural division that he rightly feared would be altogether inaudible in terms of key structure alone, since the musical continuity everywhere employs key-relationships much more distant than the tonic-subdominant relationship upon which the formal opposition is built. Of course, this was frequently the case in late Romantic music; the first movement of Brahms' Clarinet Quintet is a case in point, since its formal plan is based on the contrast between tonic minor and relative major - keys that are however virtually indistinguishable in Brahms' late style. The Brahms therefore creates an elegiac effect of lyrical spinning-out, rather than clearly delineating a musical form; whereas many of the details of Schoenberg's composition are clearly intended to clarify and underline the music's formal design. Schoenberg's characteristic view of the aesthetic process as one of communication is evident in the very language of the note he wrote on the Chamber Symphony in 1949, where for example he described how the transition to the Adagio at number 77 "shows many aspects of the fourth chords and adds resolutions into triads".[14] This use of the word "shows" - the note was written in English - is very similar to the way in which composers of the Princeton school talk about music "presenting" structural relationships, normally serial relationships of a highly abstract nature. Their approach however merely takes to an extreme limit a certain pedagogical aspect of the classical style, with its clearly articulated statements and transformations of readily recognizable materials; Schoenberg in fact commented on the "exaggerated intelligibility" of classical music as being "too ponderous for our present-day sense of form".[15] Nevertheless the assumption that the aesthetic value of music derives from its conveying clearly articulated form is common to Schoenberg and to classical music, or at least classical music as it was seen by early twentieth century critics and analysts; and indeed it is in this distinctive attitude towards form that the neo-classical aspect of Schoenberg's music principally lies.

But to what extent does "the average good listener" in practice hear music in terms of such compositional organization, or is to define aesthetic response to music in such a manner arbitrarily to ignore much of the enjoyment listeners ordinarily derive from music? It can hardly be an accident that the rise of the 'functionalist' aesthetic in music was more or less contemporary with the beginnings of music appreciation as an organized educational movement. If, as he feared, Schoenberg's listeners found difficulty following his music in the ways he apparently intended, then equally listeners found it hard to hear classical music in terms of the unitary relationships Schenker showed in his graphs. Texts such as Felix Salzer's <u>Structural Hearing</u> were written in order to help listeners to hear music in such terms. The message of these books was that hearing music in this unified manner, while not necessarily easy (indeed both Schenker and Schoenberg stressed that listening to music was never easy[16]), was possible and desirable; so that 'functional' analysis was intended not simply as a description of how listeners do listen but also as an aesthetic recommendation as to how they should listen. This brings to light a final characteristic of the conception of musical listening as involving more or less rational thought. This is that the listeners can decide how he will hear the piece, and that his experience of it can be modified by training, study or reflection: Schenker frequently poses analytical questions in terms of such decisions: by what criteria, he asks, should the ear understand this to be the main line, or that to be the tonic?[17] The implication is that if one makes the wrong decision, or if one simply lacks the necessary criteria for making such a decision, a proper aesthetic apprehension of the music is impossible. This can happen either because the music is at fault (in the example just quoted, Schenker was criticizing consecutive fifths on this ground), or because the listener is in some way unequipped to cope with it. Thus the antagonism engendered by modern music has frequently been explained in terms of a kind of historical drag between composer and listener. Books like Gerald Abraham's This Modern Stuff, addressed specifically to the 'man in the street', attempted to show that modern music was essentially no more than a logical evolution from the Romantic style, and to equip the ordinary listener with the minimal degree of technical expertise necessary to understand this evolution. According to Abraham, "if you are not prepared to tackle the difficulty of the modern idiom in the same way as you would tackle the learning of Spanish, if you decided to take up Spanish as a hobby, then you must resign yourself to the fact that modern music is not for you".[18] If in this way the actual process of musical listening, by virtue of the specific knowledge it requires, was seen as varying from one historical period to another, then equally it could be expected to vary from one geographical area to another. According to Abraham, 'Indian music ... merely sounds to most of us like normal chromatic music played out of tune";[19] without study and practice, he implies, a proper aesthetic reaction to its microtonal structures is impossible. Again, Meyer refers to "the danger of reading Western meanings and expectations into passages where they are not relevant",[20] and such belief in the mutual opacity of musical cultures has become established as a critical orthodoxy.

In this way musical listening has come to be widely seen as a process in which specific cultural knowledge mediates between the musical stimulus and the aesthetic response, and which therefore has both a geography and a history in the same way as do language or legal codes or other manifestations of human reason. And the analyst's role is seen as one of contributing to or explaining such specific cultural knowledge: on the one hand, therefore, his function merges into the critic's, in that he propounds the knowledge requisite for a proper aesthetic understanding of music where it may be otherwise lacking; while on the other hand it merges into the historian's, anthropologist's or even psychologist's, in that he uncovers the cultural knowledge actually mediating in the aesthetic reponse to music at different times and in different places. In this way 'functional' analysis combines a particular theory of listening, an aesthetic stance, and an assertion as to the role of the analyst himself. In this thesis we shall consider the validity of all three.

The perception of form in music

I

How far can people's experience of music be described in terms of the formal properties of the musical object? How far, in other words, is the 'functionalist' account of musical listening an accurate description of what goes on when people listen to music? There are undoubtedly situations where conscious, rational thought does play a significant part in listening to music and where the listener's experience can in consequence be adequately accounted for in terms of the formal elements and structures that are perceived. The most obvious of these is aural dictation as practiced in Western musical education, which is precisely a matter of making formal decisions as to what the perceptible elements and structures are; that is, of constructing an explicit representation of the musical object. This is not however simply a matter of extrapolating from primitive aural sensations; rather it involves interpreting the sound in terms of predefined musical categories - the categories built into musical notation, as well as simple higher-level categorizations such as diatonic and chromatic chords. Indeed it is often easier to determine higher-level categories and proceed from them to lower-level categorization - for example, identifying an overall I-IV-V-I sequence may help to identify the particular notes. Because specific knowledge is involved in this way, aural dictation requires training; it also requires, until the student is very proficient, conscious attention to the task. Over a period of some seconds the student may deliberate: was that a minor second or an augmented fourth? is this the same chord as the piece began with or its dominant? Conscious strategies are adopted (I'll hold on to this final chord and see if it's the same as the opening one when the piece is repeated, or I'll fix the cadences first and then fill in between). Redundancies are discovered and exploited (I know that's a strong beat, so the previous note must be a dotted crotchet). In this way the music is treated as information, according to the cognitive categories the listener brings to the task (that is, the notational symbols and so on); and when the information so defined is exhausted the task comes to an end: no more can be achieved in these terms.

There are obviously many respects in which the listening done in aural training is untypical of musical listening as a whole. Normally the listener does not exhaust the piece in this manner: people go on listening to music even when they "know it backwards"; to this extent they do not seem to treat it as information at all. Again, some music is much easier in terms of aural training than other music: it would be extraordinarily difficult to transcribe the development of the first movement of Tchaikowsky's Fourth Symphony in any detail not simply because so many instruments are playing but because the music does not fit easily into block-harmonic categories. Yet for most listeners, who have no such training, Tchaikowsky is one of the easiest composers to listen to. So again the listening done by trainees in aural dictation is untypical of that done by ordinary listeners in concert halls.

Clearly, then, we cannot generalize wholesale from the one type of listening to the other. Aural training tells us what people can do under special conditions; they may be unable to make the same identifications in the concert hall. But equally important (and this is something that applies to all experiments into musical perception), knowing what people <u>can</u> do when listening to music is by no means tantamount to knowing what they normally <u>do</u> do.[21] So the analytical validity of the 'functionalist' account of musical listening must be justified, if at all, by reference to listeners' performance under normal conditions of aesthetic relevance. Thus, how different is the perception of musical form under normal aesthetic conditions from the kind of identifications made in aural training? As in aural training, the perception of form involves an active synthesis on the part of the listener as well as the specific structural qualities of the musical stimulus; it requires that the listener experience the musical sound as delineating an aesthetic object or artefact of some kind. To hear a movement as a rondo, for instance, requires that its sections be experienced as gestalts, and moreover that a memory of some of their characteristics is retained - sufficient for the elementary judgements of sectional identity and non-identity on which rondo form is based. Typically a listener may have a sense of 'this' and 'that', or 'here and 'there' - a simple binary division of 'here we go again' as against anything else. Even so basic a scheme of listening as this imposes categories upon the musical sound, makes divisions where the sound flowed smoothly, and withdraws sections from the flow of time. Any perception of musical form thus involves the listener in an active participation in which he not only deduces relations between what he hears but, so to speak, decides what to hear. For example, if we hear the coda of the first movement of Beethoven's G major Quartet Op. 18/2 as necessitated by the eccentric recapitulation of the first subject in the submediant major (bar 170), then that E major passage becomes that much more prominent as a significant gestalt in our 'vision' of the piece; because of this we may notice such things as its relation to the E minor inflection of the recapitulatory cadencing (bar 202), making a direct but temporally removed connection which would otherwise have been swallowed up in the easy moment-to-moment continuity of the musical sound. Inasmuch as any perception of things as timeless and yet distinct from each other must be a spatial perception, to hear music as form is thus to experience it spatially, and therefore in terms of imagery that is likely to be either kinaesthetic or visual.[22] The listener distances himself from the sound, in that what he reacts to is not the sound as such but as mediated by his image of it. This 'distancing' of experienced form from immediate aural continuity is more obvious still in later sonata structures. To experience the first movement of Bruckner's Ninth Symphony or Schoenberg's First Chamber Symphony as sonata forms requires the listener to pick out the beginning of each thematic section. (This is actually very easy: Bruckner tends to stop dead before each new theme, while Schoenberg usually marks its advent with a rallentando and decrescendo.) In each case, but particularly the Schoenberg, only the initial few bars of the section are significant for the formal plan of the movement: they identify the theme and the key, and almost immediately the music develops away from both. To perceive the form therefore involves making a judgement about what labels to attach to the themes and what key they are in, and in effect ignoring the rest of the music (as far as form is concerned, that is).

To experience music in terms of form, then, means not

simply hearing the sound, but interpreting it as a token of something that is not audible as such. The particular qualities of formal listening become evident in those cases where a musical element at first heard simply as an individual sound or gesture comes in the course of the piece to be heard as a formal token of some kind: a small-scale example is the cadence onto B major in the second Ricercar of Stravinsky's Cantata, which is at first heard simply as a quasi-tonal gesture, but through its multiple repetitions begins to be heard as a token of the formal articulation of the movement into verse-like sections. Now aural training also involves hearing sounds as tokens of formal relationships which are not specifically aural but (in the case of intervals, for instance) can be represented numerically or spatially; however the particular qualities of formal perception as it occurs in normal aesthetic listening are quite distinct from those of the identifications made in aural training. The first difference between the two is simply one of scale. The 'distancing' involved in perceiving music as form takes place at a level very different from the myopic involvement of aural training. More important, however, is the nature and interest of the determinations involved. Aural training involves quite strict deduction (whether from, say, harmonic progression to individual notes or vice versa); accordingly the identifications made in aural training can be determined to be right or wrong more or less without any possibility of further argument. On the other hand in neither the Beethoven, Bruckner or Schoenberg examples I mentioned are the formal identifications beyond argument: they are to some extent arbitrary, while equally they are in some degree personal and may even involve the exercising of taste. In other words these formal identifications involve a degree of freedom absent in aural training; and for present purposes - that is to say, for musical description rather than aesthetic theorizing - it will be convenient if we define such voluntariness as characteristic of imagination rather than perception, or at least of imaginative rather than literal perception.[23]

This is not merely a matter of the impossibility of saying without possibility of argument what the formal structure is. It is also a matter of the interest with which the listening is done, and this brings to light a further distinction between (so to speak) 'musical' and 'musicological' listening. The analyst listens to musical form not, on the whole, with the aim of coming to absolutely unquestionable conclusions, but at least with the aim of making up his mind what he thinks; he aims at belief, and this could be described as a perceptual rather than imaginative characteristic.[24] But in ordinary concert hall conditions the listener is not concerned to make up his mind on knotty issues; he may hear the music formally (in the sense of the 'distancing' I described) but his interpretation of the music is not such that it would be invalidated by a counter-indication in the way the analyst's would. To describe the listener's sense of form as a hypothesis would therefore not be correct. When I hear the abbreviated recapitulations at the end of Chopin's D^b major Prelude or Debussy's <u>Jeux</u>, I do not (first) observe a particular configuration and (second) make a hypothesis as to its intended role as a token of the opening: I simply hear the music as an abbreviated recapitulation. Such perception is immediate; deliberation culminating in belief is not involved, and this again is characteristic of imaginative perception.[25]

Fugal form, too, is experienced more as an imaginatively than as a literally perceived structure. Nobody - certainly not most people - can hear all the structure (in the sense of being able to perceive the slightest 'cheating') just by listening to a five-part fugue. Instead one perceives little knots or twists of structure: an opening rhythmic figure, a shake or a wide interval that makes its way one by one through the voices - these things may even stand out in stretto, inversion or cancrizan. What however is characteristic of fugue is not the little the listener perceives literally but the much that he perceives imaginatively: for round each of these perceptual fragments there spreads a sense of logical structure leading out of the attentional field: a kind of imagined lattice of music far too complex to be grasped by ear alone. By the term 'fugal form' we mean not a particular musical structure (thus textural micro-canons in post-war music are fugal devices but not 'fugue' proper) but a distinctive combination of perception and imagination; that is to say, not simply an objective structure but also the particular type of involvement the listener has with it, an involvement which is not a direct function of the objective structure but allows the listener a degree of freedom.

We can summarize what we have so far established by saying that perceiving musical form involves a kind of 'distancing' such that the music is in some degree perceived as an object autonomous of the listener; but that the degree of this autonomy (and therefore the degree to which the response is determined by the formal properties of the stimulus) is considerably less than in the case of aural dictation - where (in this sense of 'distancing') the music is perceived as a musical object even at a note-to-note level. Inevitably this creates a discrepancy between the objective properties of the musical score and the degree to which musical sound is normally heard as an objective structure. An illustration of this, at the level of what one would normally call texture rather than form, is the issue of perceiving vocal or instrumental lines. It can be argued that to perceive a musical line at all - that is to say, a motion from one note to another - is to constitute the musical texture as a kind of imagined object. This is demonstrated by asking, with Roger Scruton, exactly what it is that moves from one note to the other. Scruton says: "We may find ourselves at a loss for an answer to that question; for, literally speaking, nothing <u>does</u> move. There is one note, and then another; movement, however, demands <u>one</u> thing, which passes from place to place".[26] Accordingly, he says, to experience a musical line as moving must involve imagination; linearity is a property of the music as an imaginative object and not simply a psychological effect that the music makes upon the listener. Now a musical score constitutes the music as an object in this way, in that it categorizes the sound into a number of distinct lines (even if each line is shown as a series of discrete events rather than an imagined motion). But how far is this the same perceptual object as the listener constitutes? Thus how many lines do people ordinarily hear in music? The answer to this question, of course, turns on what is meant by 'hear'. In terms of a specific internal representation of the sound - Schoenberg's "taking note", "remembering" and so forth - the untrained listener can probably pick out only one continuous line at a time, since he can only represent it to himself by means of an imagined singing (or possibly a visual or kinaesthetic analogue). Of course he will have some generic awareness of the other lines in a four-voiced texture, and in fact in many musical textures his attention will not be fixed on a single line throughout but will weave in and out of the texture as new voices enter or imitate one another. On the other hand a musician - by virtue of 'feeling' simultaneous parts in his fingers as on an imaginary keyboard, or 'seeing' them on an imaginary stave - can often hold four or even more lines in mind at once in a fairly specific manner: specific enough to play them or write them down (though whether he could pick them all out at a single hearing would be doubtful in all but the simplest textures.) However nobody can possibly hold in mind all the forty parts of Tallis' <u>Spem in Alium</u>; even Tallis himself must have worked it out sequentially. Does this mean nobody can hear it properly, then? The evident absurdity from the aesthetic point of view of such a conclusion shows the limitations of defining 'hear' in terms of a specific internal representation of sound. In vocal textures of any complexity the listener 'hears' the voices not so much in terms of a specific perception of each but in terms of the overall effect of their sonority and multiplicity; and this constitutes the sonic background against which a particular voice will here and there advance into or retreat from the field of attention and so be perceived specifically as a moving 'line' in Scruton's sense. To this extent experienced sound and score not only are dissimilar but, in a sense, have precisely contradictory attributes: for the listener the overall texture is given and the individual lines, if they are to be perceived as such, will often need puzzling out; for the score-reader the individual voices are given but the overall textural effect may be difficult to reconstitute.

Much the same applies to the perception of the timbrally distinct lines of different instruments; literal perception merges into imaginative perception, and imaginative perception into overall effect. There are instances where a literal perception of the instrumental lines as separate is a precondition for making aesthetic sense of a musical texture. A negative demonstration of this is Eduard Steuermann's piano reduction of Schoenberg's First Chamber Symphony, which (unlike Webern's less drastic reduction) frequently makes no sense at all to the listener unacquainted with the original; so that to hear Schoenberg's music as texturally articulated must at times involve the perception of distinct instrumental lines as a necessary mediation process, even when the listener is not actually conscious of listening to the instruments as such. More often, however, perceiving instrumental lines is not so much a necessary stage in a higher-level structural apprehension, as an end in itself: to notice the diffferent instrumental colours coming to the fore, blending, and separating in Ravel's orchestration of Pictures at an Exhibition is a source of pleasure in its own right which obviously plays no very important function in clarifying the texture since that was clear enough in the piano original; just as the perception of imitative entries in Baroque textures is rewarding in itself, creating the sense of a fine, tightly-knit fabric, rather than necessarily serving any larger formal purpose. Hence, again, imaginative perception of instruments is as characteristic of listening to music as is the literal perception of them; the one merges into the other. For example, I perceive the ondes martinot in Messiaen's Turangalila Symphony, but when (as sometimes happens) I hear voices in its climaxes I must be imagining things. I hear the guitar in Debussy's <u>La Serenade Interrompue</u> though I know it is no more real than the bells in <u>La Cathédrale Engloutie</u>. I hear the orchestra in Liszt's transcription of the <u>Liebestod</u> (though I can by way of experiment decide instead to attend to the actual piano sonority of the tremolandi: immediately the music begins to sound like a pub piano, orchestral sonority and passion both instantly evaporating). In Czerny's transcription of Rossini's <u>Semiramide</u> overture for eight pianos (thirty two hands) the illusion of orchestral sound is at times so compelling that I cannot, even if I try, hear it as eight pianos (let alone thirty-two hands). Thus it is common enough in music to 'hear' instruments that are not there. Equally it is common enough not to hear instruments that are there. Ravel's orchestration is praised for its entirely novel sounds - sounds that the listener cannot resolve into their component instruments. Again, fine pianists are praised (I have heard it of Lipatti) for creating in the listener merely a sense of the music, rather than of piano or pianist; it is as if one were removed from the place and time of the concert. This imaginative sense of being released from physical space is as characteristic of music as it is (say) of literature or representational painting; the phenomenologist Don Ihde has pointed out how a bad wrong note can so disrupt the experience of music not because it renders it incomprehensible (one usually knows what the note should have been) but because it jerks the listener back into an immediate perceptual awareness of performer and instrument.[27] In all these ways, then, the score (representing the music as a complex of instrumental events each of which might be perceived as such in isolation) is a workable symbol of the intended musical sound, without being by any means an accurate descriptive analogue of the listener's experience. That, after all, is why listening to music with the score so modifies the experience of it, enabling the listener to pick out instrumental parts – or make distant tonal connections or whatever – much more readily than otherwise. Even watching an orchestra play, as opposed to listening to them on a record, modifies one's aural perception in a comparable manner, because the musical texture can be 'seen' as a complex of specific instrumental events.

The discrepancies between the normal experience of musical sound and the way it is represented in scores or by analysts, then, arise in part from a certain personal freedom of imagination that is characteristic of musical listening, particularly at the level of form; and in part from the fact that many aspects of music (particularly at the level of texture) are heard in terms of overall effect rather than in terms of the specific structures or events that create these effects. To hear music as overall effect, however, is to have little or none of the freedom characteristic of imaginative perception. Whereas a listener can decide to pick out this or that element of musical form, and so decide how he will 'hear' or 'see' the piece, to respond globally to a musical texture is to pick out nothing in particular; so that the listener's experience is a more or less direct function of the musical sound. This however does not mean that the listener's response is a direct function of the structural properties of the musical sound, in the sense that structural relationships between different musical sounds will necessarily correspond intelligibly to the different effects these sounds have upon listeners. Consider a situation in computer synthesis. The listener hears a tone which he can merely describe generically or by some kind of external association: he may say that it has a thin, reedy sound, for instance, or that it is somewhat like an oboe. It is of course possible to give a precise recipe for the tone in mathematical terms. In itself however this does not describe the quality of the tonal experience; rather it sets the tone in the context of other tones related by various transformations of its physical parameters. In general however these mathematical associations do not correspond in a very manageable manner to the perceived associations of tone quality; steady-state spectra only allow the crudest predictions, and transients are excessively complex to calculate. Hence the fairly general lack in computer music of genuine timbral composition, in the sense of designing musical structures by means of purely timbral relationships, as envisaged by Schaeffer or Stockhausen; instead, high-level computer synthesis 'languages' like Music 4BF incorporate sub-programs to predetermine an 'orchestra' of timbral 'instruments', which execute the composed pitch, rhythmic and formal structures much as in conventional music.[28]

In general such 'instruments' in computer synthesis are designed in terms of the effect that the sound shall have upon the listener, such as the associations it evokes, so that there is no immediate structural correlation between this effect and the analytical notation by means of which the sound is to be specified. The situation is not unlike that of a parfumier who is after a more or less predetermined effect which he attempts to realize by the manipulation of the ingredients he has at hand. Now there can be little doubt that much of musical composition is done in such terms; musical textures (as opposed to forms) are in general designed in terms of an intended effect, rather than in terms of objective structures intended to be constituted as such by the listener. Indeed it could be argued that this is really what we mean by the distinction between texture and form; and furthermore, that by 'composition' proper we often tend to mean the formation of objective structures intended to be constituted as such by the listener, and not the design of sounds in terms of intended effects. At any rate it seems natural to speak of 'composing' musical forms and a little odd to speak of 'composing' musical textures. At the same time any such distinction between 'form' and 'texture', or for that matter 'composition' and 'non-composition' defined thus, is difficult to draw with precision, at least if the aim is description rather than prescription. For example, one might reasonably talk about Ligeti 'composing' the micropolyphonic textures of <u>Melodien</u>, <u>Lontano</u>, or the Chamber Concerto. Yet these textures work more or less as does the perfume we mentioned, in that it is not expected that the particular objective constituents should be specifically perceived. In the case of the perfume this is normally impossible, and even if it could be done in the case of the Ligeti - that is, if the particular polyphonic elements could be picked out in the manner of aural training - the aesthetic effect would largely be lost. The pulsating, intricate webs of texture experienced by the listener have to be perceived globally; Ligeti's compositional process apparently begins with verbal or visual models of these effects, and it is only in terms of such psychological effects that his scores usually make sense (apart from a few very obvious large-scale formal articulations or processes). The same could be said of many composite textures built up of separate rhythmic levels on the analogy of overtones as in Schoenberg's <u>Five Orchestral Pieces</u>, Debussy's <u>Jeux</u>, or Stockhausen's <u>Gruppen</u>; it could indeed be said of the tonal as well as textural design of some passages in Berlioz' <u>Symphonie Fantastique</u>, especially when the music passes rapidly through keys related by step. The music is evidently designed to create certain tensional, theatrical or coloristic effects. Viewed in terms of structural logic the score makes virtually no sense at all; indeed this is what we mean by describing the general trend towards 'coloristic' use of harmony in the course of the nineteenth century. For aestheticians like Collingwood this would be as much as to say that such music was not, properly speaking, art at all but mere entertainment. Collingwood's distinction between what he termed "Art proper" and "Art falsely so called"[29] is undoubtedly much sharper than anything that emerges either from the subjective experience of music or from observation of the public's listening habits; there is no evidence for saying that Berlioz and Ligeti appeal to audiences less interested in artistic values than those who listen to Bach. Nevertheless, the construction of music round psychological effects - which is what Collingwood means by entertainment - is particularly characteristic of Muzak (that is to say the tapes of background music produced by the Muzak Corporation for use in factories and other places of work). Alexander Goehr comments of it that "for the music to make its full effect it must be composed, so to speak, in reverse. You have to start with the effect it is intended to make and then translate this into sound material... Such a procedure flies in the face of orthodox musical teaching and practice".[30] In particular, it flies in the face of the 'functionalist' aesthetic I outlined at the beginning of this chapter and so makes analysis in 'functional' terms impossible.

II

We have, then, identified 'form' with the listener's voluntary constitution of music as an experienced object, as against his involuntary experience of it as a global psychological effect that is predetermined by the composer. (It is the way the listener experiences the music, rather than the historical fact of the composer's intentions, that matters in this identification.) We have seen that the 'functionalist' account of listening is predominantly concerned with 'form' defined in this sense, that is to say, in terms of the structure of the musical object; but also that scores represent things in terms of 'form' (defined thus) which are in practice not experienced in this manner under normal circumstances – things we would normally refer to as 'texture' or even 'sonority', but which are nevertheless very far-reaching in the music of such composers as Ligeti and Berlioz.[31] The issue that remains to be settled, therefore, is one of scale: to just what extent do listeners normally (as opposed to in aural training or under experimental conditions) hear music as form rather than as effect, and how far can this experience be directly correlated with the structural principles of the music? And in answering this question we will be by implication determining the limits of what analysis carried out on 'functionalist' principles can tell us about the aesthetically important properties of any given piece of music; or to put it another way, how much of the pleasure people normally derive from music (and hence how much of the musical design, as intended to elicit such pleasure) is necessarily excluded from our consideration if we adopt the 'functionalist' aesthetic when we analyze music.

The issue of Muzak, just mentioned, brings to light a kind of longstop in the aesthetic perception of music: that is to say, an extreme limit beyond which music is not heard aesthetically at all (or at least not in our current musical culture). There is a definitive reaction to Muzak, and to various other types of musical stimulus, which is at least as characteristic of the untrained listener as of the professional (and perhaps more so), and this is: 'that's not music!' It appears to be music that is calculated, or at any rate felt to be calculated, which excites this kind of rejection. However we must distinguish two types of calculation that are involved here. The first is when the calculation is in terms of intended effect - this is no doubt one reason why many people detest the very idea of Muzak, and there are those who dislike Berlioz or Britten for the same reason; Schenker dismissed as "ideas composers", and Adorno as "intellectualists", those who wrote music simply to convey some extramusical intention.[32] But the rejection of music as calculated equally applies in the opposite instance when the calculation involved is structural: that is, when music is (or is felt to be) calculated in purely symbolic terms without reference to its sound. The very possibility of serial music was repeatedly denied for this reason; and Charles Seeger coined the term "musicological composition" for mathematical music designed numerically and only translated into sound at the last moment.[33] Since most twentieth-century listeners to art music are neither particularly well-informed about, nor particularly interested in, the compositional process, this oddly moralistic reaction of rejection should probably be construed not so much as an aesthetic belief about how music should be composed as one about what it should offer the listener: namely, something of the imaginative freedom that we noted as characteristic of 'form' in music, and which is denied by any music that is wholly determined either by means of externally-imposed calculi, or in terms of psychological effect. Music that is wholly determined in either way is, from the listener's point of view, aesthetically overdetermined; hence the similar reaction each provokes in the listener.

This act of aesthetic rejection on the listener's part seems to represent the minimum degree to which the aesthetic experience of music does, as the 'functionalists' maintained, involve perceiving musical sound as a token of some kind of musical object - that is to say, as form. At the same time it is clear that responding aesthetically to music, in our culture at least, involves a number of factors which have little if any direct relationship to the structural properties of the music in question. Beliefs of what can only be called a moral nature are involved; the passionate reaction of rejection just discussed has all the characteristics of a moral judgement, as does the rejection of any music of which it is felt that the composer had no real control over the musical outcome in aesthetically important ways (hence the force of the various spoofs played from time to time upon audiences of avant-garde music) - for such rejection has no direct basis in the actual structural or sonic qualities of that musical outcome itself. Historical beliefs have an effect upon aesthetic perception too: the publication of Mussorgsky's original score of <u>Boris Godunov</u> must inevitably alter the way people hear the Rimsky-Korsakov version that until now has been <u>Boris</u> for all but a handful of scholars.

Even feelings of snobbery are not wholly without influence upon the experiencing of music, particularly at the formal level; or at least upon the terms in which listeners describe their experiences.

For all these reasons, as well as the freedom of imaginative perception we discussed earlier, there are serious objections to making any such immediate connection as 'functionalist' analysts have sought to establish between the structural properties of the musical object and the listener's aesthetic experience of musical form. And there is no doubt that sometimes analysts and critics use a vocabulary relating to such structural properties in discussing musical contexts where further inspection suggests that no such structural properties are in fact relevant. One example of this is the concept of musical logic. In normal usage the term 'logic' refers to a system of formal relationships, and sometimes music is indeed logical in this sense - for example, the "uncompromising dynamic counterpoint" (as Keller calls it[34]) of the Minuet from Mozart G major Quartet K.387 is strictly logical in terms of musical symbols, although the actual effect of the music is less definite. So here 'logic' refers to formal relations more or less regardless of aural effect. On the other hand the word is sometimes used of contexts where no such relationships are involved: for example the 'gritty logic' characteristic of British music between the wars was as often a matter of style (principally harmonic vocabulary, square-cut rhythm and instrumental writing) as of anything more formal. Again, the finale of Bartok's Second Quartet creates the effect of a sublime but demanding logic that almost goes beyond what can be actually rendered audible; but it does so, not by virtue of any demonstrable relationships of interval, line or temporal proportion, but through the very awkwardness and unyieldingness of its instrumental writing - for it is full of huge leaps with exposed entries in high positions and frequently <u>piano</u>: almost impossible to attack quite smoothly and with perfect intonation. In such instances the term 'logic' is being used not to refer to structural qualities but to the effect the music makes on the listener, a certain suggestion that appeals to the listener's imagination. Another example is the concept of musical proportion itself, which (like logic) is a term widely used in making value judgements about music. But what is it that is being measured when music is said to be well-proportioned? Not, clearly, clock time or bar-numbers, since universally satisying proportions can be established in neither; when used in this evaluative sense, proportion must relate to some more subjective sense of musical temporality, a sense of time that will vary according to the individual musical context. But in that case we are no longer dealing with objective relationships at all; it is difficult to avoid the conclusion that, as applied to musical forms, 'well-proportioned' is more an expression of aesthetic satisfaction than a specific explanation of that satisfaction in terms of structural relationships. In architecture, it has been pointed out[35] that whether or not a facade appears proportionate depends as much upon the detailing as upon the actual proportions themselves, so that the concept of architectural proportion is effectively devoid of content in the abstract; in the same way it seems likely that high-level explanations of musical value in terms of formal relations may often do no more than convey, in a misleadingly complicated manner, an aesthetic response to the musical details of line, harmony, texture and sonority.

The suggestion I am offering, then, is what common sense might lead one to expect: musical form as it is ordinarily experienced lies somewhere midway between the mere psychological effect of Muzak on the one hand, and on the other the highly complex transformational structures in terms of which 'functionalist' analysts have explained the effect of music upon the listener and in particular its aesthetic value. However both the experience of music itself and the words in which listeners describe their experiences are so overlaid by musical and historical beliefs, by imagination and by snobbery, that it is far from easy to determine with precision and certainty just how much objective form, what degree of structural relatedness, listeners do ordinarily experience in music. Nevertheless some strong indications can be found to support this suggestion.

When we talk analytically about tonal 'forms' we see them as working divisively rather than additively; that is, they are predicated on an overall tonal unity which they articulate in various ways through local tonal centres functioning as 'dissonances' to the overall tonal centre. (Charles Rosen for example describes modulation in classical music as "essentially a dissonance raised to a higher level".^{36}) Hence the historical importance attached to those first nineteenth-century works in which such tonal closure was set aside, such as Chopin's Second Ballade which begins in F major and ends in A minor. Consequently it is no longer possible to say what key the work is 'in', but only that in which it begins or ends (unlike, for example, Beethoven's first and last symphonies, each of which has an oblique tonal beginning but in neither of which the overall tonality is in doubt). There seems to be no reason to believe that such tonal openness either shocks or stimulates the average record-buying listener, or indeed materially affects his experience of the music at all. (Since verbal reactions are not necessarily a reliable guide, certainty about this would only be possible on the basis of experiments using versions of the Ballade reworked so as to end in F minor, in G minor and so forth.) If this is correct – as informal questioning of listeners suggests it is – then there is no reason to believe that tonal closure at this level has a more significant effect upon listeners than does tonal openness.

The purely phenomenological basis of tonal closure would seem to have two aspects. The first applies on the small scale, perhaps under forty seconds' duration. Within some such span tonal closure or its lack is immediately and reliably perceived. A version of the National Anthem which ended on the dominant would sound patently unfinished. The shortwinded modulatory excursions that return to the tonic, and that are characteristic of Bizet, Prokoviev and Richard Strauss (particularly in his later works such as the Oboe Concerto) probably extend such reliable and immediate aural perception of tonal closure to something like its maximum limit of duration. As the Rosen quotation suggested, we can see larger musical forms as designed by analogy with such directly audible tonal closure; but that does not mean that such larger forms have any directly audible tonal closure themselves, because whatever principles govern musical perception clearly do not apply at all levels regardless of duration. Indeed it might be argued that there are no specifically musical principles of structure above durations of forty seconds of so, so that above this span musical forms are built on principles shared with other arts or activities - narrative structures, for example, or formal designs of repetition, contrast and transformation that are equally applicable in the visual arts.

The second phenomenological basis of tonal closure would be the sense one sometimes has of a tonic 'clicking' when regained, especially when it has been quitted and is now reapproached disjunctly rather than by a smooth sequence of (let us say) fifths. This can happen on a fairly large scale - some minutes at least - but this sense of tonal identity is by no means wholly reliable; it is sporadic and sometimes mistaken (except for listeners with perfect pitch, of course); it can easily be confused or overlaid by a continuous and strongly argued modulation. Because this aural phenomenon is so weak relatively to the complexities of musical form, tonal music is by and large designed to shore up such structural identities of key by means of corresponding identities of theme, texture, orchestration and so forth - at least where the composer felt the experiencing of tonal closure to be formally important. As I mentioned in connection with Schoenberg's First Chamber Symphony, even textures became highly conventionalized in late Romantic music, as a further device for rendering formal articulations recognizable independently of key. Hence when a listener does experience a large-scale tonal form as closed it may well be that he is reacting not so much to precise structural relations inherent in the musical object, but to generic textural qualities which he hears as clues to the intended form.

But in any case we probably overrate the extent to which listeners do this. In part this is evident from audiences' public listening habits. In Beethoven's day it was quite normal for the movements of a large-scale work to be separated by performances of fashionable arias (as happened in the premiere of his Violin Concerto), or for movements to be interchanged between different symphonies. Presumably the development of cyclic thematicism in the mid-nineteenth century was an attempt to force a sense of organic unity upon an indifferent public. Nowadays public concerts respect organic unity far more; but at home people often enough listen to one side of a record of a symphony and then follow it by something else, or play it again. After all, missing part of a piece of music – arriving late at a concert, a break in transmission – has much less devastating aesthetic consequences than missing the beginning of a film, which may easily make the remainder incomprehensible. The unavoidable impression is therefore that many people tend to listen to music, not in an organic manner in which the relation of part to whole is paramount, but in a moment-to-moment, edge-related manner, one thing leading sequentially to another. And when a thematic link or repetition is noticed, the effect will often be simply to tie the music into a tightly-knit whole rather than to articulate its structure: the listener remembers he has heard a tune, or a striking chord or orchestral sonority, earlier in the piece, but may not remember exactly where (at least not without a conscious effort, and perhaps not even then). Consequently it would seem that many people experience musical form not in terms of the systematic and conceptual structures predicated by the 'functionalists' but rather in terms of the more basic types of cognitive organization that psychologists refer to as "heaps", "collections" or "complexes":[37] organizations of objects perceived as only partially independent of the observer, and which are perceived as related to each other merely by association or by the sharing of attributes chosen more or less at random.

A confirmation of this may be found in the forms of music that has no culturally institutionalized form, and which is therefore designed more or less from scratch on each occasion, so reflecting purely aural criteria more directly than is the case of such traditional forms as sonata. Variation sets are a good example: nothing is predetermined about their form except that it will be sectional and sequential. But any well-composed set of variations is of course designed to be more than this. Take for instance the <u>Handel Variations</u> by Brahms. Legato and staccato, homogeneous and fragmented textures roughly alternate, assuring a certain degree of superficial variety. Variations exploiting a particular idea occur in clusters, rather than in any specially logical sequence; thus the horn call which first occurs in the seventh variation recurs in the twelfth and then pervades the fifteenth to eighteenth inclusive. Again, the use of the mediant rather than the dominant in the third bar (which is anticipated by the melodic structure of the theme) first occurs in the fifth variation and is taken up in alternate variations from the ninth to the thirteenth. Underlying such surface clusters is a simple tonal plan which at first alternates tonic major and minor, only once straying from B^b to the relative minor (in the twenty-first variation); and crowning the whole is a fugue which bears no particular resemblance either to theme or variations but brings the set to a satisfying close simply by virtue of its weight. Here, then, is an 'informal' form which relies on no overall unity of organization but instead disposes the material into loosely organized complexes which share one or two particular attributes. Even the relationship of theme to variation is like this: apart from the set numbers of bars disposed in the two halves, there is nothing in common between theme and variation that applies throughout. Some variations adopt the harmonic structure of the original. Others develop one of its melodic ideas. Some (but not all) retain its pattern of repetitions. Others cannot be directly related to the theme at all, but only to other variations. In other words the theme is used, not as the seed of an organic structure in which everything can be related to everything else, but as a repertoire of ideas - a storehouse that contains musical possibilities but without any particular internal organization. We may hypothesize that this kind of informal organization in terms of 'heaps' and 'complexes' represents the irreducible, phenomenological basis of musical form as a vehicle for music content. Purely aural form, in the sense of something specifically perceived as being distinct from content, is thus simple and obvious: verse-like alternations of contrasted materials (as in Messiaen), for example, or simple processes of build-up or intensification such as are found in Rossini overtures, the Rheingold overture or Ligeti's Continuum. Complex, institutionalized forms such as sonata may derive from such a basis but they clearly augment it through the liberal use of elaborate symbolic schemes that go well beyond the limits of the purely aural. The specific characteristics of these complex, cultural forms cannot therefore be explained in terms of phenomenological universals, but only in terms of their particular historical development.

An elementary level of musical consciousness

The suggestion that most people listen to musical form at a rather elementary level is not a new one. John White, for example, has said that "as far as I'm concerned, many people listen to a lot of classical music just from phrase to phrase, waiting for the really good bit to come up, more or less switching off after the 18th Variation of Rachmaninov's <u>Paganini Variations</u> until the exciting bit at the end comes up".[38] More generally Aaron Copland has written that "from self-observation and from observing audience reaction I would be inclined to say that we all listen on an elementary plane of musical consciousness ... we respond to music from a primal and almost brutish level - dumbly, as it were, for on that level we are firmly grounded... and all the analytical, historical, textual material on or about the music heard, interesting though it may be, cannot - and I venture to say should not - alter that fundamental relationship."[39] Such an assumption certainly accounts for a number of attributes of music which are problematic in terms of the 'functionalist' account of musical listening with which this chapter began.

In the first place, conscious activity of mind hardly seems to be a necessity in the enjoyment of music. In fact Eric Blom considered listening without conscious effort as the most rewarding way to hear music; he called it "over-hearing" and defined it as "a kind of hovering on the brink of receptiveness, an absorption of the musical impression without any conscious effort. We may be keen, but tired ... But once the lassitude has worn off, we shall find that the impression has remained - nothing very definite, perhaps, only an afterglow, but something compelling and enduring just the same. It is rather a blessed state to find oneself in at a concert, and afterwards the felicity, felt to be undeserved, is perhaps for that very reason the more welcome. The only trouble is overhearing cannot be cultivated. It is a delight that comes rarely, a gift of the gods to accept thankfully, but it must not be expected too often. When most expected it will be least likely to produce itself."[40] All we can do, he adds, is to listen intently. But what exactly does listening intently involve? If I find my mind wandering during a concert I may tell myself: 'listen!' By this I don't mean, attend in any specific manner; I simply mean, don't think about other things, don't let anything get in the way, be open to the music. In this sense it is quite characteristic that people 'just listen' to music, rather than listening 'to' anything in particular. Making an effort to follow a chordal progression or a sequence of modulations is likely to do more harm that good under such circumstances, because it imposes categories upon the music which are aesthetically crude and inappropriate. Perhaps this is why major innovations in musical style (Monteverdi, Mozart, Wagner, Stravinsky) have so frequently become established in the theatre or opera house, where the audience's attention is diverted elsewhere; rather than in the concert hall where there is nothing to attend to but the music, and where inappropriate expectations on the listener's part therefore cause more damage. Certainly a wide public responded to the Ligeti works used in the soundtrack of 2001: A Space Odyssey; avant-garde styles still considered 'difficult' in the concert hall or on the radio are now quite commonplace in the soundtracks of television series broadcast to mass audiences. It is almost as if unfamiliar music required one not to listen harder (as is usually asumed), but less hard. In fact it is well known that music can have a very considerable subliminal effect, that is to say when people are making no effort to listen at all; the financial success of the Muzak Corporation is based on the premise that "music can influence the emotional state without demanding the conscious attention of those hearing it".[41] Muzak therefore reprocess music by diminishing dynamic contrasts, so that the music does not attract attention to itself; a static dynamic level is also characteristic of 'easy listening' music, which again clearly influences its listeners' state of mind (inducing relaxation and a certain effect of well-being) without requiring conscious attention.

As I mentioned, some people look upon Muzak as a public nuisance; the indignation provoked by all forms of musical interference suggests that the response to music at this level is largely involuntary. The stories of the Sirens, the Tarantella and the Pied Piper of Hamlyn all turn on the listener's inability to resist music's influence, as in our own century do the recurrent allegations that pop music diminishes the minds and morals of the young. There are admittedly all sorts of ways in which the response to music is voluntary: if (as we saw) the experience of a series of notes as a moving line is imaginative, then it must be possible for the listener to decide not to hear the notes as a moving line; though this is sometimes quite difficult, and if it is true (as Scruton maintained) that "I must be attending to what I hear if I am to hear it as a melody"[42] then the attention involved can be at a very low level. I attend to the book I am reading, but I am still vaguely conscious of the tune coming from the radio next door as a linear motion, not a series of individually static and unrelated tones. Indeed at the level of texture the perceptual characteristics of music seem to a considerable degree independent of the particular way a listener directs his attention: when listening to Berg's Violin Concerto I may decide to follow the violin or direct my attention to the orchestra, but the effect of this upon my experience of the sonority is quite minimal. I experience the sound as being almost as independent of me as a landscape over which my gaze may wander at will.

Similarly, the listener can decide to 'hear' (the inverted commas signifying, as usual, hearing plus imagination[43]) a musical form in one way or in another; and simple decisions of this sort, as in the case of Beethoven's Quartet Op. 18/2 which we discussed above, are not wholly without effect on the aesthetic qualities of the music. But it is easy to overrate the aesthetic importance of 'hearing' a musical form in one particular way as against another, and this is particularly the case where the formal determinations involved are of any degree of complexity. A case in point is the first movement of Elgar's First Symphony. The form of this movement is extraordinarily ambiguous, with its opening motto in A^b that is at first heard as a frame to the D minor exposition, but which turns out to be not frame at all but part of the actual picture, since it is the key of the second subject recapitulation. In fact nearly half the movement is in this final A^b, since the recapitulation 'overruns' and begins to retrace the development; consequently the ternary form of the sonata begins to be 'heard' as a double binary form with the coda matching the development. But 'heard' who by? The analyst and the connoisseur, to be sure; but even then I do not find my experience of the music significantly changed from an aesthetic point of view. The music seems to work in much the same narrative way as <u>The Dream of Gerontius</u>, relying for its aesthetic effect on the quality of its details rather than on the perception of its complexities of form; perhaps such an unusually complex, clever form is in fact viable just because it serves little basic aesthetic function in the music, just as in the case of the canons at a regular series of intervals built into Bach's <u>Goldberg Variations</u> which may well go quite unnoticed when an untrained listener enjoys the music in the ordinary way.[44]

Because it is only distantly related to the music's audible effect, expounding the form in such cases is not unlike literary criticism. However literary criticism is much more powerful, and culturally central, than is its musical equivalent: no critic has influenced the experiencing of music to a degree comparable with F.R.Leavis' formation of the literary response of a generation of readers. This is presumably because the aesthetic response to music is less capable of modification by argument than is that to literature; in my experience discussion of a new piece seems to exert a retroactive influence upon one's experience of it if the discussion occurs within about ten minutes of hearing the music, but otherwise hardly at all. There are admittedly occasional cases where a new interpretation allows an aesthetic response to music which was otherwise impossible: recently I was listening to a passage from Oliver Knussen's <u>Ophelia Dances</u> which struck me as muddy, somehow perverse. Then I recalled the title: of course, this must be Ophelia's madness: and with this realization the sound seemed to open up, the texture to become clear. But such instances of the modification of experienced sound through bringing specific knowledge to bear upon it (as opposed to the simple familiarization that occurs over two or three hearings) are rare, and indeed music is liable to be condemned if it requires such an exegesis; again unlike literature, where nobody thinks to condemn a Jane Austen novel simply because it presupposes the reader's having some familiarity with nineteenth century English mores.

All this would suggest that listening to music is considerably less historically sedimented than reading novels; depending less, that is to say, on specific cultural expectations and knowledge. As regards the expectations, it is quite often maintained as if it were self-evident that listening to music involves a great deal of expectation: Gilbert Ryle for example writes of someone hearing a waltz for the first time that "he does not know how this tune goes, but since he knows how some other waltz tunes go, he knows what sort of rhythms to expect. He is partially but not fully prepared for the succeeding bars, and he can partially but not completely place the notes already heard and now being heard. He is wondering just how the tune goes, and in wondering he is trying to piece out the arrangement of the notes. At no moment is he quite ready for the note that is due next. That is, he is thinking in the special sense of trying to puzzle something out".[45] The analogies between this unfortunate and Stuart Hampshire's ideal listener are evident enough; the validity of this as an account of what it is like to hear a waltz for the first time is not. As I suggested earlier, it is passivity rather than active engagement that seems characteristic of a first listening to music in an unfamiliar style; one simply lets the music soak in. The kind of active expectation Ryle is talking about seems more characteristic of a certain dissatisfaction with the music (one keeps anticipating the next interesting bit too soon, for example);or else it can be a quite conscious aspect of the experience of unusually dramatic moments - that apparently never-ending lull before the finale of Beethoven's Emperor Concerto, for instance, where I find myself repeatedly 'pre-hearing' the music (it is almost like pre-echo in a record). Again, the opening of Beethoven's sonata Les Adieux (Ex. 1.1) plays on the listener's expectation of a

Ex. 1.1: Beethoven, Sonata Op. 81a , bars 1-2

natural resolution to the horn call; the C minor is a kind of conceptual dissonance probably wasted on the vast majority of present-day listeners. But these are merely special instances where such expectations are immediately obvious. Only rarely would a 'literary criticism' of music based on them find a great deal to say that was more than peripheral to music's aesthetic interest.

As regards the specific knowledge, the ease of enjoying music without any specific understanding of how it is put together is surely one of music's most immediately striking characteristics. Concerts and recordings of mediaeval or of oriental music attract considerable audiences without there being a fully corresponding spread in technical understanding of such musics. Music does not appear to be universal in the complex, theoretical sense of sharing any but the most rudimentary phenomenological or psychological structures throughout all its historical and geographical variants; yet this is sufficient to render it very nearly universal in the simple, descriptive sense that individuals of one culture find it remarkable easy to enjoy that of another.

Where a lack of specific cultural training does however make a great deal of difference is not in listening to music but in imagining it in a manner that is on the one hand precise and on the other voluntarily modifiable. This manifests itself in two ways. The less important of these is exemplified by having a tune 'on the brain': it is because the listener cannot voluntarily modify his image of the tune that he cannot shake it off. The more important way concerns the amnesia that seems to grip musical culture. Composers write their ideas down straight away in case they forget them. (It's true that exceptional talent for composition is sometimes associated with phenomenal memory - Mozart, Schubert, Skalkottas - but it is clearly not a prerequisite.) Most solo performers and all orchestras rely heavily on scores. Listeners come away from concerts unable to summon up anything more definite than a couple of tunes - and, perhaps, the "afterglow" Blom referred to.

This apparent amnesia is in fact largely a question of recall rather than of initial memorization. Memories of pieces heard years before and apparently forgotten can be reawakened when the music is heard again. Most people must know far more music than they realize. The difficulty is not in storing the memories but in summoning them up at will. Someone without musical training is more or less impotent when trying to recollect a tune: the music either comes of its own accord, or not at all. Someone with a musical training can do rather more, however. If the sound of a piece does not immediately come to mind, a pianist may find that his hands can prompt him. Or it may come back when he recalls that it began on a C. If necessary he resorts to the score. For the musician the symbols he has been trained to use act as bridges between intention and sound. But even then there are many images and feelings that pass through the mind when music is heard, but which cannot be recollected in its absence. I once attempted, by way of experiment, to write down every least impression that struck me when listening to a recording of Ligeti's <u>Double Concerto</u> for flute and oboe. Ideas, images and associations would crowd in upon me till after a few seconds I had to switch off the music if I was to get them down on paper. But as soon as the music stopped most of these impressions disappeared, leaving at most a verbal husk or a visual trace than no longer meant anything to me. Yet as soon as I switched on the music again, the same images flooded back just as they were before. Evidently the sensory component of these images was so strong that they could hardly be grasped in the absence of the actual sound. The experiment strikingly illustrated the difference between the edge-related, associative kind of thinking characteristic of musical experience - a type of 'thought' barely independent of the sounds prompting it - and the rational, voluntary thought of the music analyst. It is almost as if two separate planes of consciousness were involved.

The varieties of musical listening

Allusions have already been made in this chapter to the fact that people listen to music in different ways and with different interests, and that there is not necessarily any logical relationship between the different ways in which music can be heard. Some of these involve the mediation of specific knowledge of one sort or another, and as a whole this applies to types of listening which are more or less at a tangent to the aesthetic effect and value of music. An example where this is obviously the case is that of the piano technician who accurately assesses the condition of an instrument by ear from playing a few notes: expertise acquired over a long period is involved here, and whereas listening in this way ultimately serves aesthetic purposes (in that it results in a better piano) it is not in itself an aesthetic way of listening to music sound. Somewhere between this and a more normally aesthetic listening lies that of the instrumentalist buff: that is, the listener whose interest is primarily in the way different performers interpet a familiar piece rather than in the piece itself. Such listening, which is characteristic of music critics as well as of many amateurs, clearly involves aesthetic values; but, because connoisseurship of this sort again requires a considerable degree of knowledge and experience acquired over a period, the emphasis of these values is different both from the way the music analyst listens (for he is primarily interested in the piece rather than the interpretation) and the way many music-lovers must, who lack any such extensive knowledge and experience. Hard and fast distinctions however are impossible: for example, it is difficult to see that anybody could derive much pleasure from the actual sound of Paganini's Caprice No. 24 when performed, since it is so difficult that even a Yehudi Menuhin could not be said to play it well; his recording of it is at times quite rough and inaccurate as regards tone, intonation and rhythm. But it is precisely the evident near-impossibility of the violinist's task that makes the sound exciting to hear, so that some perception of this (merely derived from the sight of the performer, perhaps, rather than any specific understanding of the technical problems) is more or less a prerequisite for aesthetic enjoyment. However a great deal of music predicates of the listener little or no such perception of virtuosity as virtuosity.

Similarly it is not possible to draw hard and fast distinctions between ordinary perception of musical form, analytical listening and the listening done in aural dictation sessions; but the differences of emphasis and indeed in what is actually perceived are evident enough. Aural dictation aims at demonstrable fact and is based on the quite explicit notational categories and structures learnt in the course of a musical education. Analytical listening involves categorization too, but this time of a more implicit nature: where two analysts 'see' the form of a given piece differently, it is usually impossible to make an objective determination of which is right and which is wrong, but it is at least possible for each analyst to present arguments in favour of his interpretation and for their readers to decide which way of 'seeing' the piece they find convincing. In this way analytical listening aims at belief rather than fact, and again it presupposes at least some technical familiarity with musical structure. Perception of form in normal listening, like analytical listening, involves 'seeing' the music in a certain way rather than being wholly immersed in the immediate sound; but as we have seen argumentation leading to belief is barely involved at all, and the formal structures that are perceived are not only personal and subjective, but of a much lesser degree of complexity than the analyst's account of the music is likely to be.

Different ways of listening to music, then, involve different ways of perceiving the music as an aesthetic object. It is important to realize that this does not mean that the same things are perceived in each case but rationalized differently; it simply means that different things are perceived. The ordinary listener does not respond to musical form by virtue of building up an objective image of it by means of specific determinations such as are made in aural dictation; conversely the aural trainee does not need to respond aesthetically to the music in order to transcribe it correctly. No hierarchy of function, therefore, is involved between these different ways of listening to music: they operate, so to speak, in parallel rather than in series. Equally it is hard to justify seeing the different ways of listening to music as constituting a hierarchy of aesthetic legitimacy, as does for example Theodor Adorno;[46] his account of the most "fully adequate" way in which music can be heard is not unlike Stuart Hampshire's description of the aesthetic process in music, involving as it does a specific 'recomposition' of the music in terms of its overall formal structure - and therefore corresponding much more closely to the structural image built up by an analyst over a series of hearings, rather than the more immediate and carefree involvement of the ordinary concertgoer or record-buyer.

'Functionalist' analysts explained, and continue to explain, the aesthetic value of music in terms of complexities of formal structure which are not perceived as such by most listeners, in the sense that there is no determinable correlation between formal structure and aesthetic response. This can be justified simply on the grounds that music is by nature an elitist art; Schenker, according to whom "an unbridgeable chasm has always existed and will continue to exist between art and the people",[47] would presumably have done so. Such a position is perfectly tenable, though it leaves entirely unexplained the enjoyment that most people do, as a matter of fact, derive from listening to music. On the other hand, if we do wish to understand this, then we cannot accept the 'functionalist' analyst's account of musical structure as having a great deal of immediate application to the normal aesthetic experience of music. Such analysis is not a description of what people ordinarily experience. Indeed to analyze music is quite specifically and deliberately to detach oneself from ordinary aesthetic listening. It is to step quite outside the flow of musical time, since all analytical listening involves recollection and the inter-relating of events recollected;[48] it involves making rational and voluntary determinations to a far greater extent than normal listening; it involves to a far greater degree the mediation of symbols which vary from one musical culture to another, in a way that the possibility of responding with enjoyment to musical sound does not seem to. It is through a series of concrete examples, however, that the distinction between analytical listening and ordinary aesthetic listening can be best made.

One such example is attempting a precise analysis of something like an Ornette Colman improvization. The music is very difficult to grasp in terms of conventional notation not only because it is extremely fast but also because it is full of little glissandi and microtones; at first hearing one responds to it emotionally and sensually, but with very little precise sense of its detailed structure and design. Through a series of listenings, however, it is possible to build up a somewhat schematic image of the music which relates fairly directly to its objective structure (as mediated by the notational categories) and which may even bring to light structural regularities not otherwise apparent; as the analysis proceeds, a kind of 'parallel piece' evolves in the analyst's imagination, becoming increasingly visual and controlled. Yet as soon as the analysis is put aside and the record played again, the music is re-experienced just as it was in the first place: at the basic level of emotional and sensual response it has been virtually unaltered by the passage of time or by intellectual reflection.[49]

Admittedly this Colman example is an extreme case of the disparity between the immediate reponse to musical sound and the mediated image of analyst; but it is by no means an isolated instance. It is hardly less true in the case of Schoenberg's Piano Piece Op. 33a. The serial structure of this piece, viewed analytically, is elegantly designed; quite apart from the usual hexachordal combinatoriality of Schoenberg's mature serialism, it gives a different harmonic coloration to the various segments of the whole and allows veiled allusions to tonal functions. But whereas the serial design unfolds itself stage by stage to the analyst, the actual sound of the music remains stubbornly opaque to the listener attempting to familiarize himself with it. However often I listen to it I never seem to get far beyond a generic impression of the sort of sound you are bound to get if you play enough notes far enough apart and at sufficient speed. At most a few passages become familiar by dint of repetition - the opening chord sequence, the 'song-like' second subject, the high chord that twice initiates a phrase in the development.

Again it must be admitted that the Schoenberg example is not wholly typical, if only because the piece is not very satisfactory and hence no analysis of it can be very satisfactory either. But a worthwhile analysis of a good piece will often create the same sense that there are two pieces (the ear-piece and the image-piece) running side by side; that, for example, is how I hear W.J. Mitchell's Schenkerian analysis of the <u>Tristan Prelude</u>.[50] Mitchell not only 'analyzes out' most of the specific aural details which, for many, <u>are</u> the <u>Tristan Prelude</u> (the curiously shrill woodwind sonority at bar 12, the constant slipping from A minor to A major by reinterpreting the C as a B#, and so on); he also discovers, or invents, a through-composed linear skeleton that relates everything by a direct harmonic relationship to the overall A minor tonality. Both in its specific, musically-notated 'inner counterpoint' and in the functional continuity of its tonal relationships, Mitchell's account of the music goes well beyond anything I find immediately audible when listening in the ordinary way. But it's exactly for this reason that his analysis allows me to 'see' the Prelude, so to speak, in a single ray: that is, to escape from its immediate temporal flow as a series of sensuous effects and so experience it, to a much greater degree than is otherwise possible, in formal terms - for a Schenkerian analysis as much creates a 'formal' apprehension of music, in the sense of a timeless synthesis on the listener's part and a distancing from the immediate musical sound, as do traditional 'formal' taxonomies of the Prelude in terms of exposition, recapitulation and so forth. Of these matters more will be said in Chapter Four.

In this way the analyst's account of music is far from being a neutral analogue of what the listener experiences in the ordinary way; but it is in the discrepancies between the two that much of the value of a musical analysis lies, precisely because it makes it possible to 'hear' the music in a way otherwise impossible. As the inverted commas suggest, what characterizes analytical listening is the degree to which imagination is involved, and the degree to which such imagination is rational in the sense of being under the listener's voluntary control. The contrast between the ordinary listener's experience of music and the analyst's account of it is in fact merely an instance of the more general contrast between listening to music and imagining it.

Notes

1: The Gypsy in Music, p. 308-9.

2: Theory of Harmony, p. 29.

3: This term has never been a precise one in musical analysis, and I use it here much as Meyer defines in in Music, the Arts and Ideas, p. 294 ff. I am not therefore using it as an antonym for structuralism (as does for example Seeger: Studies in Musicology 1935-75, Chapter 7).

4: Modern Writers and other Essays, p. 174-5. Another statement of the same view is R.G. Collingwood's: as in a lecture, says Collingwood, so in music "what we get out of it is something which we have to reconstruct in our own minds, and by our own efforts; something which remains for ever inaccessible to a person who cannot or will not make efforts of the right kind, however completely he hears the sounds that fill the room in which he is sitting". Collingwood even adds that "any concentration on the pleasantness of the notes themselves concentrates the mind on hearing, and makes it hard or impossible to listen" (The Principles of Art, p. 141). There is thus a strong link between 'functionalism' in music and the traditional distinction of 'aesthetic' pleasure (which is interpreted and hence imaginative) from 'sensuous' pleasure (Scruton, Aesthetics of Architecture, p. 71-2).

5: Fundamentals of Musical Composition, p. 1; Style and Idea, p. 103.

6: The Musical Experience, p. 98.

7: Music, the Arts and Ideas, p. 291.

8: Quoted in Samson, Music in Transition, p. 223.

9: Structural Functions of Harmony, p. 19.

10: Ibid, p. 195.

11: See for instance Forte, in Yeston, Readings in Schenker Analysis, p. 20; Rothgeb, Some uses of Mathematical Concepts in Theories of Music, p. 208 ff.

12: E.g. Forte, in Schenker's Free Composition, p. xx.

13: Style and Idea, p. 61.

14: Note on the First Chamber Symphony, reprinted in the booklet to Columbia Records, The Music of Arnold Schoenberg Vol. III, p. 33.

15: Theory of Harmony, p. 128.

16: Free Composition, p. 9; Style and Idea, p. 103.

17: Free Composition, p. 57; similarly Schoenberg in Style and Idea, p. 123.

18: This Modern Stuff, p. 22.

19: Ibid, p. 59.

20: Emotion and Meaning in Music, p. 107.

21: Davies, Psychology of Music, p. 40.

22: For this definition of spatiality, see McDermott, A Conceptual Music Space, p. 490. Thomas Clifton observes that if one describes Webern's <u>Bagatelle</u> for Cello and Piano Op. 9/1 as in cyclic form, then "what have I been talking about, if not a visual experiencing of the sound-structures of this Bagatelle?" (<u>Music as a Constituted Object</u>, p. 86).

23: Scruton, <u>Aesthetics of Architecture</u>, p. 86, 90.

24: Ibid, p. 87.

25: Ibid, p. 77.

26: Ibid, p. 81.

27: Ihde, <u>Listening and Voice</u>, p. 79. Sartre describes the same jolt on leaving the concert hall: <u>Psychology of the Imagination</u>, p. 225.

28: Howe, <u>Electronic Music Synthesis</u>, p. 205 ff.

29: Collingwood, <u>The Principles of Art</u>, p. 275-6.

30: <u>Musical Ideas and Ideas about Music</u>, p. 10.

31: In his analysis of the Webern Bagatelle mentioned in n. 22, Thomas Clifton observes that "once the twin idols of pitch and interval are overthrown, this problem of sonority becomes more pervasive than is generally acknowledged. It seems that here, Webern takes great pains to minimize the importance of pitch and interval (as meaning-objects), so that what is perceived contributes to the 'field of presence' ... in the form of a sonority which, at any given moment of the Bagatelle, provides us with, as it were, the same cross-section in a more or less concealed manner" (<u>Music as a Constituted Object</u>, p. 92).

32: <u>Free Composition</u>, p. 9; <u>Philosophy of Modern Music</u>, p. 1

33: <u>Studies in Musicology 1935-75</u>, p. 128.

34: <u>The Chamber Music</u>, p. 110.

35: Scruton, <u>Aesthetics of Architecture</u>, p. 67 ff.

36: <u>The Classical Style</u>, p. 26.

37: The terms are Vygotsky's (<u>Thought and Language</u>, p. 59 ff).

They apply to stages of cognitive maturation. If listening to music involved conceptual thinking, we would expect to see radical changes in the ability to listen musically at various set ages. This does not seem to be the case; with some exceptions, chidren appear to enjoy much the same music as adults (thus there is 'children's music' but it is not nearly as well-defined a category as is children's literature). It is true that evidence has been found of a maturational development from perceptual to conceptual dominance (Sergeant and Roche, Perceptual Shifts in the Auditory Information Processing of Young Children), but this is based on tests of singing memorized tunes. As will become evident in Chapter Two, all sorts of factors mediate in performance which have no role in listening, so that direct generalization from singing to listening is not well founded.

38: Quoted in Studio International, November/December 1976, p. 237.

39: Music and Imagination, p. 13.

40: An Essay on Listening and Performance, p. 739.

41: Publicity material, Muzak in Industry, from Planned Equipment Limited.

42: Art and Imagination, p. 179.

43: Ibid, p. 108.

44: Formal complexities of an extreme sort are thus found in what, from the viewpoint of aesthetic effect, are 'free spaces' - for example, the kind of textural polyphony that Nono or Lindholm calculate systematically (by series and canon respectively) but which Ligeti apparently does not - at least I have never found a system in, for example, his Chamber Concerto. Aurally it makes no difference whether the texture is systematic or improvized.

45: The Concept of Mind, p. 216.

46: Introduction to the Sociology of Music, p. 4-5.

47: Free Composition, p. 106.

48: See Schutz, Fragments on the Psychology of Music, p. 30-2.

49: The image built up under these circumstances clearly depends on the analyst's expectations. I conducted some tests in which students attempted such a transcription. The sequence of their attempts revealed exactly that influence of cultural prototypes and gestalt 'goodness' familiar from Gombrich's <u>Art and Illusion</u>: they would begin by assuming metric regularity, tonal closure and so on and only succeeded in revising these initial assumptions to a limited degree and that with difficulty. The important point, however, is that their aesthetic response to the music evolved in no such manner but was essentially fixed from the start: so that the cultural and intellectual mediation involved in thus representing the music as overt form was quite tangential to the aesthetic experience itself, in a way in which (according to Gombrich) it is not in the aesthetic experience of pictorial representation.

50: <u>The Tristan Prelude: Techniques and Structure.</u>

Chapter 2:

Imagining music

The general properties of musical imagination

Imagination probably plays as large a role as perception in the activities that make up a musical culture. Ordinary people imagine familiar music as they carry out some tedious task. Composers make a profession out of imagining unfamiliar music. Conducting involves not only (as is often said) a clear image of the sound that is wanted at a given moment, but also the ability to 'hear' a little in advance of the orchestra's playing - an imaginative rather than literal perception, therefore. Even the most basic problems of musical performance concern imagination: the difficulty in playing a Bach two-part Invention, for instance, is not really one of the physical movements of the hand but one of imagining the music clearly enough - hence the role of advice along the lines of 'no, you should think of this as a group of three plus four' in actually making a passage easier to play: it alters, not the sound nor even necessarily the physical movements of performance, but the pianist's image of the passage.

The distinction between perceiving and imagining tends not to be greatly respected in ordinary talk about music, however. For example, it is normal to talk of a composer like Britten having a fine 'ear' for orchestration: meaning, not so much that his perception of actual sounds was better than other people's, as that he had an unusual ability to imagine sounds (in this sense, Beethoven retained a fine ear even when stone deaf). The most obvious distinction between musical imagination and literal perception, then, is that when music is imagined no stimulus need necessarily be physically present. But in that case what does it mean to talk about imagination when there is actual musical sound present? Here, as we said in Chapter One (p. 40 above), the word denotes the essentially voluntary nature of the experience. The listener may consciously decide to 'hear' the music as an imaginary ballet, or as a battle-scene, or in shades of green; alternatively he may drift into 'hearing' the music in such a way, but he can still cease doing so at will. Without ear plugs, however, he cannot shut out all perception of the sound, or indeed some degree of response to it (if only one of irritation). If then the degree of voluntary control over what is experienced is the principal criterion in distinguishing imaginative from literal perception, then equally this voluntary quality serves to define the imagination of music when no sound is actually present. In the terms I adopt in this chapter, then, imagining music does not include hypnagogic imagery - those extremely vivid images of music that can occur on the borders of dream, but over which no precise control is possible. For this reason hypnagogic imagery, and indeed dream itself, play a fairly marginal, if picturesque, role in the formation of musical culture (instances such as Tartini's and Stravinsky's dreams come to mind); whereas imagination proper is central to it, as being the main medium in which music is designed.

The principal issue of this chapter is how far the imagination functions simply as a neutral medium for musical sound, much like a high quality sound reproduction system, and how far it imposes characteristics of its own upon what is imagined. Consider the temporal element, which is highly constrained in real, audible music (in the sense that arguments about rubato, rhythmic incisiveness and the rest take place within narrowly defined limits as to what constitutes acceptable performance). It is of course possible to 'think' a passage of music strictly in accordance with the time of musical performance, for example when a composer of 'moment-form' music 'thinks' through a section with his eye on his watch in order to check that the lengths of each 'moment' seem right. However imagining music in such a literal tempo is by no means the norm. When looking through a piece I do not always read every bar at a steady pace: I may skim over a section whose effect in performance is primarily rhetorical, and conversely my understanding of the music is not greatly disrupted when a passage is complex and I have to reread a bar, or take it slower - modifications that would create a disastrous impression in performance. Again, when I 'think' music while writing it out, I have to slow it down to the pace of my pen; the tempo becomes more or less subjective, so that it would probably make no sense if played out loud. In both these cases the tempo was distorted for a practical reason, but it is equally characteristic of casual, unconstrained imagination. Sometimes, while reading a novel for example, I will find that I have been vaguely thinking over a particular moment from a familiar work: the rarefied boy soprano's phrase before the choral cadence in Allegri's <u>Miserere</u>, for example, or the opening phrase of the second subject (in A major) from Bruckner's Ninth Symphony. How have I been experiencing the time of these examples? Clearly the image I savour is not without a rudimentary temporality, because although my image of the Bruckner is centred on the climax at the beginning of the fourth bar (Ex. 2.1) I sense this as a consequence of what has come before: there is equally a sense of before and after, a basic temporal irreversibility,

Ex. 2.1: Bruckner, Ninth Symphony, second subject

in my image of the Allegri. But this temporality is, so to speak, qualitative rather than quantitative: to assess just how many seconds this note takes, or that, is to force upon my image an objectivity it does not possess.

The deconstruction of musical time in such an image is like the deconstruction of space often described by phenomenologists: I 'see' a thimble or a lamp,[1] but although my image is visual it possesses properties denied to literal perception - so that at the same time I 'see' the interior of the thimble as well as its outside. In a similar manner, imagined music can possess a kind of completion and clarity real music does not. Quite a number of people claim to derive a more vivid experience of music from reading a score than from attending a concert. "If I want to listen to a fine performance of Don Giovanni", said Brahms, "I light a good cigar and stretch out on my sofa."[2] And even someone who lacks the musical education to read a score may nonetheless experience vivid and compelling musical images, and not necessarily of music he has heard but equally of music he has invented for himself: some golden melody, let us say, against a background of lush harmonies and all clothed in a luxuriant orchestral sonority. If only I could put such images down on paper, such a person may feel, I would be a composer: that must be how it's done.

But there is an illusion here,[3] as our would-be-composer will quickly find if he sets about realizing his image. Even assuming that he finds it possible to pick out the melody with one finger on the piano (and in the course of this he may well discover that he has to make decisions about details that never arose in the image), he will very probably find it thin and impersonal when he actually hears it out loud: not what he intended at all. And as for the harmonies and the orchestral sonority, it will prove impossible to write down exactly what was imagined, because the image was rather one of lushness and luxuriance than of specific harmonies or orchestral colours such as might in real life create such an effect. The generic effect of the harmony and orchestration was imagined, but specific sounds were not. Accordingly the image cannot be transcribed into musical notation, because there is nothing specific to transcribe. The situation is analogous to having a tune 'on the tip of the tongue': on one occasion I could not recall the Dance of the Reed Flutes from Tchaikowsky's <u>Nutcracker Suite</u>: all that came to mind was an image of its lightness and frothiness combined with a perfumed quality. These attributes converged upon Tchaikowsky's music, so that I had a very definite sense of what it was I couldn't remember; I even had a kinaesthetic sense of the pirouette at the end of its first phrase. Even so, they were not specific: I still could not remember the tune.

When people who lack any training imagine music, then, their images are more or less restricted to what can be literally sung or danced (a simple, not-too-ornamented melody, a homophonic rhythm) supplemented by a generic sense of everything else. Because this sense is generic, it entirely lacks the massivity and resistance of real, audible music. By this I mean that all sorts of generic qualities can be imposed upon the musical image that are incapable of actual musical realization. This is a general property of imagination, but one whose results are best seen when musically trained people make mistakes in imagining music. It is perfectly possible to imagine a passage of Baroque counterpoint in which the top two lines cadence on I and the bottom two on V and which yet sounds consonant and stylistically correct - but only when 'heard' in the imagination, of course. Seeing my mistake, I will 'hear' the jarring of the dissonance. But this only shows the extent to which such a jarring is a generic attribute I impose upon the imagined music, rather than something which so to speak comes out of the music itself, as when it is played.

The apparent richness and clarity of imagined music is therefore in part an illusion because what is imagined is an as-if richness and clarity rather than specifically rich and clear musical sound. Something of the the inherent poverty and incompleteness of aural imagination is perhaps made audible when people half-sing along with a record, or when they whistle at work; or most of all in the way children sing when otherwise occupied. In such cases anybody who happens to be listening will hear the thinness of tone, the exaggerated rubato, the tendency for longer notes to be abbreviated in relation to shorter ones, the pitch may drift, or the tune suddenly go into another key when its tessitura becomes inconvenient; there are arbitrary repetitions, too, whose effect can be exasperating or simply incomprehensible to the listener. But singing of this sort is not intended to be listened to: it is not even really heard by the singer, which is why it is so subjective and so musically vague. It is subjective in just the same way as children's instrumental playing tends to be: their teachers constantly urge them to listen to their playing, to hear it as if it were somebody else playing. The advice has an effect precisely because of the shortfall between imagined sound, which is vague and intentional, and actual sound, which is precise and explicit in the constraints it imposes.

If this account of imagining music is correct, then the question arises how music is possible at all, if it is based on the composer's ability to imagine sound in a highly specific and detailed manner. The answer, of course, is that composers employ imagery not shared by untrained listeners; imagery which plays an important role both as an analogue of actually heard sound and as a substitute for it, and which moreover is a major element in the formation of musical style.

The musician's imagery of sound
Though we talk about a composer's 'aural imagination' the actual imagery involved is not itself aural; what is aural is rather the synthesis of these images in the imagination as an intelligible structure. As we have seen, sound can be imagined by virtue of purely aural imagery, though in a more or less vague and generic manner: but even this becomes virtually impossible when the music is actually heard, the perception of real sound as it were crowding out the purely aural imagery of sound.[4] When a conductor has an imaginative sense of the music that is to come a few seconds in advance of the orchestra's playing, he does not have a distinct sense

of there being two musics (the audible and the imagined), nor does he have to stop listening to the actual sound in order to imagine what is to come; rather he employs imagery which is not itself aural but derives from other sensory modes, and which therefore does not interfere with the hearing of actual sound. A simple exercise to demonstrate this is the attempt to imagine one piece while listening to another. There is no great difficulty in 'seeing' the extension of the imaginary piece as a large-scale form, for example, or even in recalling something of its orchestral colour or emotional tone. But to imagine the music in any detail against the interference of the audible sound is only possible through something like the visual imagery of notation, or the kinaesthetic imagery of playing the piano. And it is imagery of this sort - imagery belonging to other sensory modes but brought to bear upon musical sound - that is equally involved when the imagined and perceived music is the same.

Such imagery may belong necessarily to another sensory mode, as in the kinaesthetic sense of playing the piano or the physical sense of tightening and relaxing the throat as one 'sings' one's way in silence through a Verdi aria; or it may be based on symbols that can equally be represented in a number of modes - as the beginning of a bar, for example, can be presented visually in the score, kinaesthetically in the conductor's gesture or the tapping of the player's foot, or aurally as when a performer counts a number of bars' rest in unconducted music. Such independence of the purely aural mode means that imagery of this sort has some degree of logic and coherence independently of sound. The symbols of musical notation embody quite complex logical structures (for example, the respective chain and circle of Pythagorean and equal-tempered fifths); of more practical importance are the various topological structures of bodily imagery based on performance.[5] The simplest of such bodily models of sound is that derived from the voice, a continuum from low to high; a little more complex is the kinaesthetic imagery derived from playing an oboe or flute, where this continuum is gradated into semitones and, at a further level, into octaves (at least in the lower registers). The guitar instils an imagery of musical sound which combines harmonic staticness (because of the constant return to open strings) with a purely chain-like sense of ongoing harmonic relations that derives from barré playing in high positions, where it is quite possible to get 'lost' when improvizing except by reference to open strings, or by looking. On the piano each key within the octave has a unique configuration in terms of black and white, up and down, so getting 'lost' is not possible (or at least likely) in quite the same way; besides, the keyboard is conveniently visible throughout, which means that relationships between (say) different keys can be seen at a glance. Planning tonal excursions of some complexity is therefore more readily done at the piano than on a guitar.

Logical and topological structures of this sort extend the purely aural imagination of musical sound because they can be grasped and manipulated in their own right; they allow the creation of a kind of imaginative web that underlies what is actually heard, much in the same way as the back of an embroidered fabric shows a tangle of threads that form no part of the design as such but were necessary in bringing it into being. In the same way performers and composers work on the reverse side of the musical fabric,[6] carefully worked-out patterns of fingering underlying the pianist's apparently effortless performance, for instance, or deliberately calculated modulatory sequences underlying the rise and fall of excitement in the Symphonie Fantastique; but though these tangles of symbols reinforce and extend the purely aural image of sound, they represent it only in an incomplete and schematic manner. Consequently though the symbols themselves are not aural, the structures into which they are organized are in general only intelligible in aural terms; to try and make sense of an image of music in purely symbolical terms would be like trying to make sense of the pattern made by the threads on the back of the embroidery without taking into account the design of the front. Two illustrations will establish this general point about images of musical sound as well as exemplifying musical images in operation: the first concerns the memory images used in the course of musical performance, while the second concerns the way people interpret symbolic structures when reading music from the score.

When someone performs a piano piece with which they are very familiar their memory of the music appears quite seamless, and may in fact be so in the sense that they know it in a number of distinct but overlapping ways — the properties of the sound, the feel of it on the keyboard, the look of it on the printed page and so forth. As in abnormal psychology, the organization of musical behaviour can often only be deduced from what happens when it is disrupted: in this case, when the music is half forgotten. Some years ago I learnt to play Debussy's Danceuses de Delphes but had more or less forgotten it in the intervening period. Trying to remember it I recalled only that it was in B^b major; that it began with a rising pattern beginning on the fifth degree which was repeated immediately and that the entire phrase was then repeated with elaborations (bar 6); that this was followed with a high falling phrase over a low note, also repeated but this time transposed (bars 11, 13); and that it ended with sustained chords. Sitting down at the piano, my hands found the first chord easily enough and I played (Ex. 2.2). Here the image involved was probably partly aural and

Ex. 2.2

partly kinaesthetic; vague enough however that the dotted-note chromatic rise had become detached from its inner line. A still clearer example of such deconstruction of the music into component parts happened in bar 3, where I played (Ex. 2.3). Clearly the abstract idea of parallel thirds had

Ex. 2.3

stuck in my mind, but I went wrong in my attempt to reconstruct these fragmentary memories into viable music. Similarly when

I reached bar 11 I recalled the initial mirror-transposition but tried to take it too far, so playing (Ex. 2.4). Again,

Ex. 2.4

I remembered the move to the flat side at bar 13 but took this too far, coming to a halt as proper continuation became impossible (Ex. 2.5). These few examples are perhaps suff-

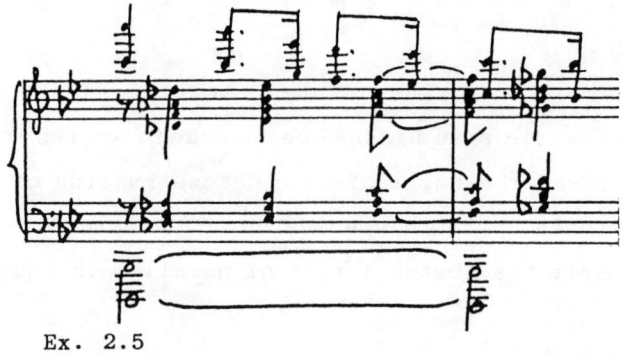

Ex. 2.5

icient to indicate the part abstract symbols play in reinforcing and elaborating the memory of musical sound; the experiment also showed the role played by kinaesthetic imagery, since it was only as my fingers moved on the keyboard that specific details of the music returned to me. At the same time these images were only fragmentary and often unclear considered in purely abstract or kinaesthetic terms. What allowed me to make sense of them was the musical sound through which I experienced them, modified them, and so reconstructed something approximating to Debussy's piece. To have reconstructed the music from these symbolic traces using a silent keyboard would have been far more difficult and perhaps impossible.

What this suggests is that to imagine music in any detail involves deconstructing it into symbolic organizations of a more or less diverse nature, whose reconstruction and interpretation requires the mediation of musical sound (real or imagined). Certainly this applies to the reading of musical scores, which must be the principal means by which people imagine music in detail – and in particular, the principal way in which people learn to imagine it in detail. Here the score itself represents a deconstruction of sound into elementary units of notation (that is to say, notes defined in terms of pitch, time, loudness and timbral classifications). What is involved in this transition from physical sound to musical score will emerge in the next chapter (p. 144 ff. below). Our present concern however is with the process of interpreting such notation that goes on when scores are read. Now it is of course possible to read scores simply by taking in the formal relationships that hold as between symbolic units; that is what old-fashioned counterpoint teachers did, who merely interpreted the music according to formal rules and hence developed remarkable skills in spotting even the most subtly hidden consecutives. The extent to which this can be done purely in terms of symbolical relationships, rather than through an aural synthesis, is shown by the comparative ease of doing it within earshot of a radio playing different music. Similarly, if one attempts to read (for example) a Haydn quartet while within earshot of a radio, it is easy enough to sort the texture into tunes and accompaniment, grasp the figuration patterns, pick out the chords, even sense the tensional shape of a period which moves towards the dominant but sidesteps to cadence in the tonic. All this can be done by eye. And this kind of symbolical reconstruction of the music is characteristic of the first few seconds of reading a score under normal circumstances. After those few seconds, however, a practised score-reader begins to read in a rather different manner. He reads more fluently and evenly, and at the natural speed of the music. He follows the main tune, perhaps with a sense of singing it to himself, taking in the cello line as he reads and so grasping the direction of the harmony (it is hardly necessary to be sure of every chord): he 'sees' the texture of the inner lines and is always watchful for the unexpected thematic interjection or harmonic twist the second violin or viola may introduce. Fluent reading of this sort is hardly possible when there is interference from other music, because although the notational symbols are not aural to read them fluently requires an aural synthesis. Hence, too, the sense of sonority that wells up after the initial few seconds of score-reading: the image develops depth and colour and other attributes of experienced sound – only to loose them abruptly, maybe, when a harmonic progression is misread or a clef overlooked, so that the reader has to return to the initial puzzling out of what the chords are or how the texture works.

Within limits it is possible to read music creatively in this manner, in the sense that the reader responds with appropriate aesthetic reaction to tunes and chords (and even, perhaps, orchestral combinations) that he has not previously encountered; responds to them, that is to say, in more or less the same way as he would on hearing the actual tune or chord or orchestral combination. The limits are however quite severe, because the aural synthesis of the score I have described is still generic in a number of ways. For example, to 'see' a texture means little more than to recognize the sound quality of that sort of texture; when I read (Ex. 2.6)

Ex. 2.6: Scarlatti, Sonata in E major, K.380 (Longo 23)
I impose upon my image the familiar quality of rapid repeated notes on the harpsichord; when the score shows oboe and flute playing in octaves in a fairly high texture I impose a Rossini-like sparkle upon my image of the sound. And this means that beyond a certain stage my reading of new sound-combinations will become merely speculative; I can get something of the effect of Stockhausen's <u>Zeitmasse</u>, for instance, from the score but my reading of it is vague and inaccurate, while in the case of <u>Gruppen</u> it is worse still. My situation is different in degree rather than in its basic nature from the one-finger pianist I described in the previous section; my image of the sound is still in part subjective, so that miscalculations are inevitable if I venture too far beyond those textures or combinations of which I have had actual experience.

Creativity, in this sense of the reader's ability to reconstruct sounds he has not previously experienced, is of course much greater in certain respects when the score is not read in silence but at the piano. The piano sound has the 'resistance' imagined sound lacks; a dissonant chord will sound dissonant when played even if the reader does not expect it to, provided only that he depresses the correct keys. In this way the possibility of interpreting each note in the score simply as a direction to play a certain note constitutes a calculus independent of the performer's ability to predict what the note will sound like. Imagination is not strictly necessary in playing a piano score at all; just as it is a purely mechanical manner to encode such a score for automatic reproduction by a computer synthesis programme, so in theory any piano piece can be performed merely by depressing given keys at given times. For a human performer, however, to do this is prohibitively difficult in all but the simplest musical contexts. As piano teachers know very well, sight reading (and particularly transposing at sight) involves breaking down the music into textural and harmonic units in much the same way as does reading a score in silence; except that there is a change of emphasis, such that for example it becomes less important to grasp a given fundamental harmony (a VI or whatever) and more important to take in the particular bass note even at the expense of a very clear understanding of its harmonic function. In other words there is a greater procedural element in reading a score at the piano: knowing, not exactly how it will sound, but exactly what to do.

Nevertheless to read music at the piano does almost invariably involve imagining its sound, even if slightly vaguely as regards pitch. This is shown by the considerable difficulty people initially find in performing music when what they hear conflicts with their performance; for example, when monitoring a tape recording so that there is a delay of half a second between performance and sound. Under such circumstances it is necessary to fall back onto symbolic yardsticks of some kind: counting one, two, three to oneself and hitting the notes at the correct divisions of the beats, for example. Inevitably such performance sounds stiff and unnatural for most music; much as does a Chopin waltz when performed in strict time by a computer. This stiffness shows that, whereas music is notated by means of pre-established yardsticks of metre, dynamics and pitch, it is not performed by means of such yardsticks; not at the detailed level at least. The performer's ear is the only practical arbiter for fine control of tempos and dynamic level in a Chopin piano piece, or for intonation in violin performance. Indeed at this detailed level the phrasing and intonation of any chamber group involves both aural imagination (singer and accompanist coordinating a <u>rallentando</u>, for example) and aural perception. A string quartet can only achieve good, or indeed tolerable, intonation if each player accomodates his playing to his partners', rather than to any theoretical yardsticks (equal temperament, Pythagorean intonation and so forth).[7] In this sense it is a straightforward description of performance practice to say that virtually all chamber music is collective improvization, differing from jazz improvization in degree rather than in basic nature. And this means that the score of a Mozart quartet plays essentially the same role as does that of a jazz composition consisting merely of a repeated riff or harmonic pattern and a set sequence of solos; each gives the performers approximate instructions as to what to do together with some indication of the desired effect. The difference is merely that the Mozart score goes considerably further before handing over responsibility to the performer's ear. But in both cases aspects of the musical sound that may be quite crucial for the aesthetic effect of the music - such as precise intonation - are left entirely unspecified by the score.

In the fine control of pacing, dynamics and intonation, then, no symbols mediate between performers, or for that matter between performers and audience: what players do by ear audiences judge by ear, so that at this level musical sound is an almost wholly public medium (in the sense that an individual performer has little privileged knowledge of what he is doing over and above what others can hear him to be doing).[8] Where the mediation of symbols is required in musical performance, then, is when pacing, dynamics or intonation cannot be judged by ear but must be measured against some external yardstick; that is to say, when the music is organized in ways that make no immediate sense in purely aural terms, or that are simply too difficult to handle in purely aural terms. For example, I count out aloud or tap my foot when trying to master a tricky rhythm; these bodily motions becomes yardsticks against which I measure my performance. Another obvious example is the coordination of rhythmic textures where each line has no distinct audible relationship to other lines, the texture making aural sense only as a whole: <u>Gruppen</u>, for example, could not possibly be coordinated simply by ear: instead each player synchronizes his performance with the conductor's beat, so that as regards rhythm the instrumentalists are not playing together at all, but only each with the conductor. Since the performance can only be coordinated through the mediation of the conductor's gestures, it is organized by means of a hierarchy of symbolic communication in the real time of the music; and there equally exist hierarchies of musical organization outside such real time, most obviously in the chain of command from composer through a variable number of intermediaries (arranger, editor, copyist) to performer. In all these cases, symbols are pressed into service precisely where the unaided ear falters.

The role conventionalized symbols of sound play in communicating musical intentions between different people is generally obvious enough, because the symbols themselves are overtly present - on the music paper, or in the dance the conductor performs before the orchestra. Their function is less obvious when individuals imagine complex music in a precise, procedural manner, but it is just as real and the function fulfilled is the same: namely, working on the back of the musical fabric by organizing it in terms which bear no immediate relationship to the listener's experience and which play litle if any direct role in the listener's aesthetic response to music. For example, when one listens in the normal way to an unacompanied folk song or a four-part fugue there is no particular reason why one should have any sense of either being in any particular key. And one can 'think' through the folk song in highly specific terms - 'singing' it to oneself, for example - without any sense of its being in one key or another, because at this level its organization is entirely audible. But if a musician 'thinks' through the fugue, even casually, he is almost certain to find himself imagining it in a particular key (or at least in a definite key-area: D, A, and E major for example all being fairly similar in terms of pianistic imagery), simply because so much of its note-to-note organization cannot be precisely grasped in purely aural terms. Indeed this would probably apply to any four-part texture, if it is to be imagined in any degree of detail. Consequently 'calculation' in terms of abstract symbols, and hence organization in terms that cannot be immediately grasped by an untrained listener (or even sometimes by a trained one), is not confined to extreme cases such as Ars Nova music and total serialism; it is quite normal in musical composition. In fact it is arguably an indispensable component of the compositional process - one of the things we mean by the term 'musical composition'.

Composition and prediction

Because composing music is primarily a matter of imagination, it is rarely a simple matter either of juggling with actual sounds or of calculating them in wholly abstract terms. Both play a role in composing but a mainly peripheral one. Most of the work of composition involves combining attributes of both. Thus, as the example of tape-delay showed (p. 96 above), it is possible to manipulate musical symbols without reference to sound; but in composition as in performance the role of symbols is usually as an aid or vehicle for imagining sound in aural terms - as in the case of four-part fugue, where the key imagery did not replace aural imagination but supplemented and reinforced it. When composers silently manipulate musical symbols in imagining music, therefore, their 'calculations' are in general as much aural as abstract, so that they would be impossible if there were musical interference from some nearby source (except in the case of exceptionally codified styles, or certain mechanical elaborations of texture and so forth).

However composing is not always done in silence; as often as not it involves manipulating actual instruments. Now one of the reasons for doing this is of course the empirical 'resistance' of actual sound, such that for example when a composition is checked through at the piano unintended effects (say a sudden tonal coloration in an atonal style) may come to light: the actual sound of the piano has a completion that the subjective 'sound' of the imagination inevitably lacks. However it is quite possible to hear piano sound in a subjective, incomplete manner. For example it is possible for the composer to miss the unintended effect when he plays the piece through, because he hears the sound as he intended it to be; it may be only when he is sitting in the auditorium listening to someone else playing it, perhaps years later, that he will perceive his miscalculation. And although in this instance it has worked against the composer, the ability to hear actual sound in a subjective, imaginative manner is an important part of the craft of composition, an ability moreover that is not particularly easy to acquire; student composers working at the keyboard tend to throw sonorities together too literally when composing for piano because they do not sufficiently 'distance' themselves from the sound, and Gerald Abraham has even criticized Schumann for remaining too closely tied to literal pianistic sonority and texture in this way.[9]

Just what does it mean to hear sound in a subjective, imaginative manner? Essentially it means ignoring certain attributes of the audible sound and 'hearing' it in terms of imagined attributes. For example, a composer may be working at the piano, making noises that strike a casual listener as quite unintelligible. But when the composer says that he's working on an adagio for strings the listener may suddenly be able to make sense of the piano sound, because he now imposes upon it (as does the composer) the qualities of sostenuto string sonority. And to do so involves ignoring the decay of the piano tone, the percussive brilliance of its upper register, and so on. Using actual sound in this imaginative manner is very similar to the way architects use actual plans or models to think buildings out or discuss them with clients. Certain perceptual aspects of the model are negated: its diminutive size, the balsa-wood texture and so on. Instead it is 'seen' in terms of concrete or brick texture, or the client may 'see' its walls as first painted one colour and then another as he makes up his mind which he would prefer. The model thus functions as a vehicle for the visual imagination, which however has a certain degree of 'resistance' or creativity in that the appearance of the building can be tested from angles the architect may not have fully anticipated, or alternative distributions of the windows tried out. In this way many decisions about the final appearance of the building can be taken empirically before actual construction has even begun.

In the same way, when working on a piece at the piano a composer is treating the piano sound as a model of the intended sound, so that many decisions about design can be taken early on in the compositional process. For this to be possible the music must be capable of making some sort of empirical sense even in its incomplete state. For example, almost all the major compositional decisions in a classical symphony can be taken on the basis of piano sound, that is to say before orchestration even begins; the orchestral sound is so to speak 'bracketed' out. Again, the music can be checked through as a harmonic reduction, which may make deficiencies of progression plainly audible which were hard to pinpoint in the full piano version; so here the music as it were speaks out when melody, texture and (in part) time are 'bracketed' too. Consequently the composer can predict what will sound good in the finished work on the basis of what sounds good in the reduction; that is to say, by ear.

In classical music there is a whole chain of stages of incompletion each of which represents a functional model of the intended composition - 'functional' in the sense of constituting a vehicle for an imaginative hearing of the piece, while at the same time empirically testing certain aspects of it. The most obvious form this chain takes is that from harmonic reduction to piano reducton to full score; these are possible, though by no means necessary, stages of the compositional process (in fact harmonic reduction is generally used as a test of what has already been composed rather than as a means of initial composition, rather as an artist may turn his painting upside down to see how its composition looks). Another such chain is textural: generally from melody though the addition of harmonic parts followed by detailed figurations and orchestration. What is significant about this in classical music is not simply that the music can be formally deconstructed this way, but that it continues to make aural sense when deconstructed. For example the exceptional degree of formal and thematic integration characteristic of Beethoven's more serious symphonies was no doubt made much easier to achieve because the music could be worked out in great detail merely in terms of a single tune plus the occasional addition of a second part. The <u>Eroica</u> sketches[10] for example shows how many large issues could be settled through trial and error in this manner; once the single melodic line had been got right there was no reason to expect trouble in its textural elaboration (which was no doubt presupposed, generically at least, in Beethoven's image of the melodic line), and in fact the final single-line version corresponds closely enough to the finished score.

Another type of chain between model and completed composition concerns time. A very noticeable characteristic of classical music (and one which is not shared by much twentieth century music) is that it continues to make a great deal of aural sense when played extremely slowly; for the pianist this is very convenient when it comes to practising difficult passages, since even when they are played at quarter speed they can be heard in terms of the intended harmonic evolution (whereas hardly any of Messiaen's piano music from <u>Vingt Regards</u> onwards works when played slowly). This also means that compositional problems can be attacked or textures elaborated in microscopic detail, without recourse to purely mechanical calculi; the music remains audible as music throughout the entire process. The reverse is also true: that is to say, classical music also continues to make sense when played or imagined faster than it is intended to go. The adagios of Beethoven's piano sonatas (Op. 2/2 and Op. 7, for example) were obviously thought through at a higher speed than they are meant to be performed: hence the curious way that they sound constantly on the edge of rhythmic and textural fragmentation. Much more importantly, classical symphonic compositions frequently make sense when thought through much faster, in terms of long-range lines and progressions that can rarely if ever be perceived as such in normal listening. They are designed rather like massively expanded phrases of counterpoint, with large scale harmonic and cadential rhythms corresponding to the immediately audible harmonies and cadences of the counterpoint, with modulations taking the place of immediately audible dissonances, and with slow registral lines that magnifiy the immediately audible melodies in the same way.

Such hierarchical relationships of small and large scale structure are of course the particular preserve of Schenkerian analysis, the underlying idea of which is that the laws of voice-leading are applicable not only at the immediate level of species counterpoint but at every level at which music can be experienced.[11] Schenker himself seems to have seen this as a psychological or even phenomenological principle universally true of all legitimate music. It is however much easier to see it simply as a type of imagery by means of which music can (but need not be) imagined on the large scale, and which has been prevalent at certain historical times but less so at others. If composers 'think' music largely by singing it through in the imagination like this, then it is natural enough that even orchestral music tends to be designed by analogy with vocal models. This is not merely a matter of small and large scale; it is also a matter of texture and register. In vocal music careful control of upper register is quite essential because the sonorous effects of the various voice-types change very rapidly as they reach the top of their tessitura: an important form-defining element in Stravinsky's Les Noces, for example, is the upper register of the choral sopranos, which rises through high A's (rehearsal number 79) to B's (number 130) - a large-scale registral relationship which is aurally quite marked because of the extremely prominent tone quality. In instrumental music however such registral control is much less aurally critical, because instruments have wider and more homogenous registral ranges. Nevertheless Schenker analysis shows how in many instances (though not in others) the top register of orchestral or piano music is as carefully controlled as in vocal music, even though its effect upon the listener must be much less marked. In such cases it seems reasonable to say that the instrumental music is being designed by analogy with the literally audible properties of vocal music, and this is confirmed by the more general tendency of music to function in the same tessitura as the voice, higher and lower registers being used principally by way of elaboration or extra colour - a tendency which is by no means necessary in purely aural terms and which is sometimes wholly controverted. So the vocal prototypes discovered through Schenker analysis should probably be seen as models of musical sound - models which make more or less no sense viewed in the abstract (thus to play through a Schenker background on the piano allows virtually nothing of the effect of the foreground piece to be predicted) but which can be used as a vehicle for an imaginative 'hearing' of the individual piece, and which may to some degree have been so employed by the composer.[12]

Classical music shows a perhaps abnormal degree of continuity between different levels of all the chains between model and completed piece I've described - from harmonic reduction to full score, from tune to entire texture, from the small scale of harmonic progression to the large scale of formal evolution. The flexibility classical music gained because it was possible to 'hear' it by means of such reductive models was perhaps won at the expense of some richness of harmonic and textural vocabulary; in certain ways classical music seems to have been tangential to the main development of harmony and texture that passes more directly from the later baroque to the mid nineteenth century. At any rate, the converse is true; that is to say, as harmonic usages broadened in the later nineteenth century and into the twentieth, so the relationship between the reductive model of sound and the effect of the completed composition tends to diverge. More than previously, twentieth century music tends to be composed either by juggling around with actual sounds (or concrete images of sounds), or else by increasingly abstract calculi.

In fact these two alternatives are closely linked, and this is conveniently illustrated by the example of Skryabin. Working as he was at the frontiers of contemporary harmonic language, Skryabin evidently thought largely through the medium of his hands at the keyboard. This can be illustrated by a comparison of the Fifth Sonata with the Trois Morceaux (Op. 52) which immediately preceded the Sonata and which are in effect studies for it. The harmonies and the melody of the second subject of the Sonata (bars 119 and 120, Ex. 2.7) can

Ex. 2.7; Skryabin, Fifth Sonata, bars 119-20

both be found in the first of the Trois Morceaux, but separately (bars 6 and 17 respectively: Ex. 2.8); and in each case the pitches are identical rather than transposed. There is of course no very pressing aural reason why they should crop up in the same transposition; the reason is doubtless

Ex. 2.8: Skryabin, <u>Trois Morceaux</u>, bars 6-7, 17

that Skryabin knew them primarily in terms of a given hand position on the keyboard. Again, the first of the Preludes Op. 74 is made up of a small repertoire of chord types which appear in a limited number of transpositions and which are bound together by a top line that simply crawls up and down in conjunct semitones. Are we to imagine Skryabin puzzling the music out on the piano, guided by hand and ear (as is evidently the case in the fourth of this set of Preludes)? Or did he calculate the piece, as its exploitation of aggregates invariant under transposition at the tritone would suggest, and as is possibly the case in the third of the set (which exploits the same invariance in a fully octatonic context); and as is obviously the case in his Seventh Sonata, which is the first piece to require of the analyst, if not a note-count, then at least a transposition-count?

The point is that in both cases - the music thought out by means of hand-positions at the keyboard, and the music thought out in silence by means of set-transpositions and aggregates - symbolic structures are being manipulated in their own right rather than as vehicles for the imaginative hearing of the intended piece. In other words reductive models are still being used in the compositional process, but it is no longer as easy to 'hear' the music through them as it usually was in the classical style. In consequence irrevocable decisions about the final form of the music are taken at a rather early stage in the compositional process, and details have to be composed more or less 'blind' on the basis of such earlier decisions. Examples will clarify this. The proportions of a classical piece are hardly likely to have reached their final form in advance of the material; at least, that is what Beethoven's sketchbooks would on the whole suggest. By contrast, Bartok, who calculated the proportions of his later music by means of the Fibonacci series, must have determined the overall proportional plan at an early stage and was then bound to it; there are whole passages in the <u>Music for Strings, Celeste and Percussion</u> that give the impression of having been written rather mechanically merely so as to fill in the previously defined form. A more striking example however is serialism, which requires wide-reaching decisions to be taken very early in the compositional process and hence limits the degree of detailed interaction possible between composer and sound (especially since accurate prediction of the sound of dodecaphonic harmonies tends to be difficult anyhow). Thus on the one hand large scale decisions are taken by means of schematic models of some sort, and on the other note-to-note continuity is worked out on the piano or through calculation; the imaginative interaction between sound on the large and on the small scale which was so easy in classical style is almost impossible in serial music. In fact as a means of predicting the aural effect of a compositional decision serialism is both crude and unreliable. The works of the total-serial period which made the most impression upon the public - Boulez' <u>Le Marteau sans Maître</u>, for example - seem to have done so mainly because of qualities having very little to do with the particular serial structure: in the case of <u>Le Marteau</u>, such typically French qualities as clarity of outline and a certain ceremonial aloofness somewhat remeniscent of Debussy's <u>Trois Chansons de Bilitis</u>, coupled with the exoticism of its fragile, tinkling textures. Nor is it only in the extreme case of total serialism that this disparity between compositional and experienced structure occurs.

In a letter to Josef Rufer, Schoenberg wrote "It will not often happen that one obtains a perfect series which is fit for use as the first immediate conception. A litle working-over is usually necessary. But the character of the piece is already present in the first form of the series".[13] The implication is that subsequent composition constitutes a discovery or clarification of what is already previsioned, whether consciously or not, in the series or basic shape; the essential characteristics of the final music are determined in the 'precompositional' properties of the series, as George Perle puts it.[14] But although a series may be precisly definable in systematic terms (offering various possibilities of partitioning, transpositional invariance and so forth) the way a serial composer uses it is rarely so systematic. (Hence the drastic differences in personal style with which, say, Schoenberg, Webern and Stravinsky handle a series.) Taking again the example of Schoenberg's piano piece Op. 33a, a number of aspects of the piece are clearly built into the series. Some are relatively superficial, like the conjunct fourths used to characterize the second subject. The main serial device used to characterize the musical form is however partitioning: in the first subject the series is predominantly split into groups of four, as against six (second subject) or three (development); and the series is so designed as to give very different harmonic colorations to each of these. The musical form is also articulated at a more structural level by the plan of serial transpositions, the excursion of the development being matched by the 'modulation' from the initial coupling of P-0 and I-5 to P-2 and I-7; returning via P-7 and I-0 to the original coupling of P-0 and I-5, which is regained at the recapitulation after the cadential phrase in bar 32. All this is of course prefigured in the hexachordal combinatoriality of the series. Moreover, the particular ordering within hexachords makes possible the ingenious way in which the initial 'modulation' in bar 27 is infiltrated (Ex. 2.9). In the right hand there is a pun on the trichordal near-invariance of the first hexachord of P-0 with the second hexachord of RI-5, with the A^b and G exchanging positions. This serves to introduce, first, the use of individual hexachords (rather than complete series) in the next few bars and, second, the fourths configuration E^b-A^b-D^b which blurs or eases the 'modulation' at a fourth from R-0 to I-7 - especially since the quartile trichords of R-0 and I-7 are placed side by side.

To derive the composed music from the formal properties

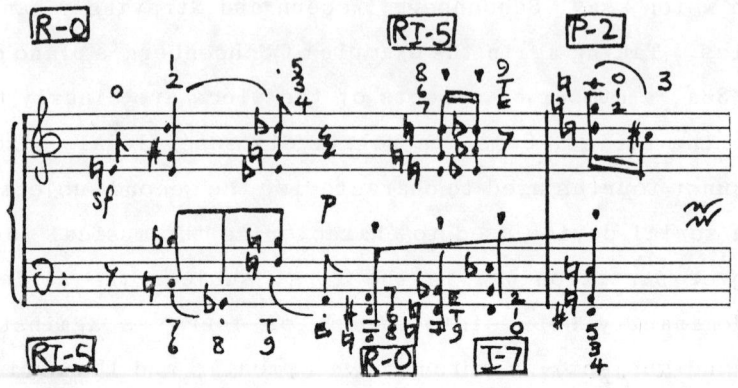

Ex. 2.9: Schoenberg, Op. 33a, bars 27-8

of the series in this way is to suggest that the series, as a reductive model, does allow the final outcome to be predicted. However there are all sorts of ways in which the actual handling of the series is unsystematic, quite apart from the few instances of 'cheating' (irregularities of ordering in bars 12, 29 and 37; the omission of the last two notes of R-0 in bar 20; the A of bar 22 and the B of bar 35, which are perhaps misprints). Thus there are, inevitably, systematic properties of the series that are left unexploited, such as the transpositional invariance of the first tetrachords of P-0 and I-2. And conversely there are methods used to articulate the musical form which have nothing to do with the serial system - notably the very traditionalistic textures of the assertive first subject, the feminine second subject, the fragmentary and discursive development, and the ritenuto-a tempo patterns that mark each formal articulation. As a predictive device, then, the series of Op. 33a is a blunt instrument, especially since most of the serial niceties I have discussed make far less impression upon the average listener than the formal associations of conventionalized textures. It would be easy to conclude therefore that to compose in the serial manner more or less inevitably means miscalculating of the musical effect, not in the sense of arithmetical errors being made in the calculation but in that an inappropriate calculus of musical effect has been adopted in the first place.

However to see the series simply as a calculus for correctly predicting musical effect is an error, and a particularly unfortunate one since it makes the widespread use of systematic devices in twentieth century music impossible to understand. If by way of experiment one writes imitations of Op. 33a, designing different series to achieve the same kind of effect, it becomes evident how little of the specific musical detail is determined in the precompositional system. Instead, as the work proceeds, the limitation of note-to-note possibilities represented by the series has the effect of imposing a specific form upon musical intentions that are often vague, or of suggesting particular formal possibilities whose aural results may only be vaguely or speculatively anticipated until tried out at the keyboard. Sometimes a possibility arising out of the serial structure will meet with a decisive rejection from the composer, and this rejection serves to clarify what it is that is wanted. Far from predicting the musical outcome from the start, then, the serial structure serves to stimulate improvization on the composer's part: unforeseen ideas or configuration suddenly seem 'right', resulting in what Alexander Goehr has called "automatic writing"[15] - stretches of music being rapidly written out almost on the basis of whether they look right rather than by virtue of an exact sense of how they will sound. Here, then, the medium by means of which the musical sound is conceived has a major creative role to play in determining the finished composition - even though this medium may have only an indirect and fragmentary relationship to the musical sound itself.

At such times a composer is working on the borderline between purely aural imagery and purely abstract calculation, using the series not as a predetermined system but as a sparring partner in a confrontation whose outcome can hardly be known in advance, or (to change the metaphor) as a vein that can be mined without knowing exactly what may be found. And this kind of working out is by no means restricted to the twentieth century. A very similar process can be seen in the Beethoven sketchbooks. Nottebohm commented of the <u>Eroica</u> that "the first sketches have in themselves little or even nothing at all of Beethoven's peculiar style and individuality; in fact they are often very ordinary and conventional. And yet they are, as it were, the soil in which the seemingly insignificant took root and bore fruit". Consequently in Beethoven "the creative faculty ... often rose to its greatest heights only at the last moment."[16] Beethoven evidently did not compose at his best in a vacuum. The rather pedestrian melodic invention of the initial sketches serves to create increasingly definite situations, to delimit compositional problems in the approach to some formal locale, and so to stimulate the characteristic last-minute improvization in which the actual music of the <u>Eroica</u> is suddenly composed. Such cases as the end of the exposition of the first movement[17] show how little of Beethoven's composition was simply a matter of transcribing what was heard in his 'inner ear'. At the same time, they show that it was not a matter of logical and systematic development of what was predetermined in any initial idea of the piece. Instead, the composition proper seems to emerge from the very shortcomings of the ideas or schematic models of the music that he played about with for so long; shortcomings that served as a stimulus for the creation of actual music where there were previously only vague intentions.

Serialism has repeatedly been criticized as being contrary to the laws of perception (or of sound, nature, etcetera). It should now be clear that this is a wrong-headed charge. Serialism should not be seen as a scientific theory of musical perception, in the sense of allowing musical effects to be precisely predicted on the basis of formal operations; as we have seen, it is as much the discrepancies as the parallels between formal operation and experienced effect that composers take advantage of in their use of serialism, as of the various other reductive models of musical sound discussed in this chapter.[18] The 'serial system' is not therefore the same sort of thing as the 'tonal system' in the sense expounded by theorists such as Matthew Shirlaw - that is, a body of scientific principles believed to govern tonal composers' procedures even though they were unaware of them as such. Instead, the 'serial system' is a technique for imagining music consciously adopted in twentieth century Europe; if there is to be a parallel betwen serialism and tonality, then the series should be compared not to the 'tonal system' but to tonal form. The institutionalized forms of tonal music constituted a vein that tonal composers consciously mined in much the same way as twentieth century composers have consciously mined serialism. As I argued in the previous chapter, tonal forms have only a fairly rudimentary foundation in the properties of perceived sound, and this too is clearly true of serial structure. The aural relationships of identity, seriation, retrogression and inversion on which serialism is based can only be literally perceived to quite a limited degree.[19]

Imagination as a stylistic and historical factor

The attempt to reduce the musical systems adopted by composers to psychological or other natural principles results from ignoring the role of imagination as an independent factor in musical culture; imagination, that is, in the wide sense that encompasses all the images or models by which music is represented, whether these models are overt (as in the case of notation) or not. Returning to the question posed at the beginning of this chapter, it should now be evident that such models do not function as neutral proxies of musical sound but impose their own characteristics upon it to a considerable degree. It should also be evident that these characteristics are considerably at variance from those of musical listening, so that it is always easy to imagine (or even compose) things that are difficult for the listener to make sense of, and sometimes difficult to imagine (or compose) things that are easily understood by the listener. Of course, not all the music that is written is necessarily convenient to imagine, just as not all the music that is performed is necessarily convenient to perform; but the ease with which things can be represented by means of cultural models must exercise a considerable normative influence upon a musical style, and probably a greater influence than in the case of, say, painting.[20]

There are two differences between painting and music that are relevant here. The first is that painting is, on the whole, a solo production in which no communication between different people is involved. On the other hand making music is, on the whole, a social production which requires efficient communication between participants (composer, conductor, instrumentalists). As we saw, where the unaided ear fails such communication relies on cultural symbols (notation, conductors' gestures and so forth) and hence on the musicians possessing a common understanding of their interpretation; and this imposes a certain traditionalism upon music, or at least a certain practical resistance to innovation, of a kind that does not really arise in the case of painting. Furthermore paintings are chosen, both by collectors and hanging committees, on the basis of their actual appearance; whereas new music is generally accepted for performance (or rejected) on the basis of the score. Inevitably this must influence the development of musical style in the direction of such literary values of formal unity and so forth as are favoured by the score, as against those more impressionistic qualities of sound that may be just as effective in performance but are almost imperceptible in the score. The second difference between painting and music is rather more subtle. In painting there is, or at least can be, a continuity betwen initial sketch and final product. The design can be sketched onto the canvas, played about with, blocked in, altered, overpainted. Each stage of the painting process is easily reversible and merges into the next; the design is present as an immediately visible object throughout the entire operation, so thst empirical decisions may be made by eye at every point. To this extent imagination is hardly involved, for much of the time at least. In music on the other hand it is hardly possible even to point to a particular point except by means of some symbolic mediation (the second subject, or there in the score, or two minutes into the piece, or whatever). And similarly the transitions between initial sketch and final product are much more complex and more sharply defined; even when a piece in the classical style is being worked out by ear at the piano, for example, it takes a certain degree of specific knowledge and experience to 'hear' the sketch as a reliable model of the intended music (a knowledge of how orchestration and figuration transform the qualities of piano sound, for example); and when composition is being done by means of working silently on the score, the role symbolic models play in composition is obvious. Musical composition is therefore bound to be affected by the characteristics of these reductive models, and the conditions that their use imposes, to a greater extent than painting, which conversely is likely to be determined to a higher degree by expressive or literary (as well as representational) intentions.

In fact the techniques of musical imagination (in the wide sense) can be considered as one of the main determinants of musical style. As I said, imagined sound is subjective and incomplete in comparison with audible sound. To design music that is fit for listening to requires that it be imagined many times over from, so to speak, different angles; each incomplete in itself but complementing the others. When composers plan out music they will sometimes concentrate on the overall form as a kind of imagined object, visualizing its structure and proportions; in doing so they more or less ignore the particular characteristics of the content for the time being. On other occasions they will be working on the musical content on a note-to-note basis, taking the overall form as read. In each case one aspect of the music is imagined in detail at the expense of the other. The same applies to the division between structure and ornamentation: ornamentation being what the composer 'brackets out', perhaps leaving it to the performer to work out the details. Probably any musical culture in which music is designed to high degree within the imagination (as is the case in Western music) must exhibit distinctions of this sort. But the particular substance of such distinctions varies from one historical (or geographical) style to another. Ornamentation is both more limited and less codified nowadays than it was in the baroque period. The classical distinction of form and content has largely disappeared with the widespread use of 'unique forms' in the twentieth century, the precompositional role of form (as I suggested) being taken by serial or other systematic structures, or by texts, programmes, numerology and the like; furthermore the harmonic, piano and other reductions that make sense in some styles (but not others) constitute further distinctions between what can be treated as 'form' and what as 'content' (or what as 'structure' and what as 'ornamentation') in any given context. So one aspect of musical style is the variety of distinctions between what is musically essential and inessential when the music is 'seen' from a particular point of view, and the particular substance of these distinctions. A second aspect has to do with the general conditions under which such reductions are intelligible as representation of musical sound. This is particularly clear as regards such 'theoretical' principles as the invariance of octaves in harmonic relationships. Whereas the dissonance-resolution pattern of a V^7 - I works reliably in the central register of music, regardless of particular pitch level, its effect is quite different and perhaps unpredictable when extremely high or extremely low, especially in unfamiliar timbral combinations. Equally harmonic progressions whose effects are familiar at normal tempi will be perceived as hardly more than a splash of colour at extremely rapid tempi, and as a series of unrelated chords at extremely slow tempi. The patterns of expectation by which one 'thinks' a tonal texture, or reads it in the score with some assurance of its sound, therefore presuppose normal registration and normal tempi. In fast tempi these patterns of expectation have to be modified, mainly by omission; the difference between Elgar's and Brahms' fast music is that Elgar wrote fast music whereas Brahms tended to write <u>tempo giusto</u> music with a high metronome marking - hence its clogged harmonic rhythms and textures. And in very slow tempi it may be more or less impossible to rely on normal models of sound at all; instead the music has to be composed almost entirely empirically, through trial and error.

Musical culture is therefore not only a function of what sounds right but, equally, of what is convenient to imagine; and whereas what sounds right seems fairly universal (hence, as I said, the ease of enjoying mediaeval or Indian music without special training), the particular ways in which music is imagined vary greatly from place to place and from time to time. In fact it could be argued that music has much more history in terms of how it is imagined than in terms of how it sounds: the 'breakdown of tonality', for instance, is readily intelligible as a breakdown in certain ways of thinking about music, whereas it seems to have a less clear denotation purely in terms of musical sound. There are after all atonal-sounding passages in Chopin and tonal-sounding passages in serial music; assigning a date to the breakdown of tonality is almost impossible if it is considered purely as a sonic phenomenon. On the other hand, assigning a date to it is straightforward enough if we mean by it a sense of dissatisfaction with the perfunctory way late romantic music begins and ends on a tonic that seems otherwise irrelevant; and the consequent search for other explicit principles of organization capable of serving a roughly equivalent function (serialism, Skryabin's chordal prototypes, Messiaen's modes of limited transposition and so forth). Seen this way, it makes good historical sense to regard Schoenberg's Fourth Quartet as much more 'modern' than Strauss' Elektra; even though a casual listener, judging merely by the sound, would very likely say the opposite.

Notes

1: Sartre, Psychology of the Imagination, p. 105. My account of imagination is largely based on Sartre.

2: Quoted in Schutz, Making Music Together, p. 174 n. 24.

3: Cf. Ehrenzweig, The Psychoanalysis of Artistic Vision and Hearing. Sartre calls this the "illusion of immanence".

4: The phenomenologist Don Ihde discusses the general principle that something cannot by simultaneously perceived and imagined in the same sensory mode. He illustrates this by the example of a yacht: with eyes closed I have visual imagery of its form, its whiteness and so forth, but this disappears when I open my eyes and see the real yacht (Listening and Voice, p. 128-30).

5: For a detailed descriptive account of such bodily imagery and jazz piano improvization see Sudnow, Ways of the Hand, especially pp. 61-80.

6: This image is drawn from Merleau-Ponty's description of the writer (<u>Phenomenology, Language and Sociology</u>, p. 42).

7: See Davies, <u>Psychology of Music</u>, p. 59-60.

8: The mutual interaction between performers and listeners described in this and the preceding paragraph was the subject of Schutz' article <u>Making Music Together</u>.

9: <u>A Hundred Years of Music</u>, p. 57.

10: Nottebohm, <u>Two Beethoven Sketchbooks</u>, p. 50 ff.

11: <u>Free Composition</u>, p. 5-6.

12: Such employment of aural imagery of singing as a background to the actual music is a sophisticated correlate of the 'inner singing' characteristic of many exotic musics - varying from the wholly conceptual melody that the Balinese term 'lagu' (Sutton, <u>Concept and Treatment in Javanese Gamelan Music</u>, p. 72 ff.) to the audible semi-song that one sometimes hears in jazz performance or ethnic music.

13: Rufer, <u>Composition with Twelve Notes</u>, p. 94-5.

14: <u>Serial Composition and Atonality</u>, p. 8 n. 12.

15: <u>Musical Ideas and Ideas about Music</u>, p. 9.

16: <u>Two Beethoven Sketchbooks</u>, p. 97, 98.

17: Ibid, p. 68-71.

18: Thus Pousseur writes that "the divergence between serial procedures and the perceptible result is sought after and exists effectively" (<u>The Question of Order in New Music</u>, p. 99).

19: For an experimental verification of this see de Lannoy, <u>Detection and Discrimination of Dodecaphonic Series</u>. This perhaps throws some light on the pristine sensitivity to tonal structure critics sometimes impute to classical audiences: Walker, for instance, writes that "by the very nature of things tonality is no longer so true for the modern listener whose aural experience is not so vivid as that of his classical counterpart" (<u>A</u>

study in Musical Analysis, p. 152). Would not a Walker of two hundred years from now equally write of serialism not being so true for the modern listener as it was in the twentieth century? It is hard to see how the music theorist can step outside the experience of music so as to make such judgements; Max Meyer was surely correct when he wrote "How can we know what Bach or Beethoven or Mozart meant except by experimenting upon ourselves, assuming that the general psychological laws of melody applied to them as they do to us?" (in Esper, <u>Max Meyer and the Psychology of Music</u>, p. 188).

20: Normativity of this sort is sometimes interpreted too deterministically. The attempt to make an immediate correlation between aesthetic response and physiognomic imagery, as was once common, is one example of this, and leads to obvious absurdities. The same perhaps applies to more modern theories correlating the psychophysiology of pitch perception with musical style. That integer-related frequencies are treated in a privileged way at the basilar membrane, as is currently believed (Creel, Boomsliter and Powers, <u>Tone Sensations as Perceptual Forms</u>, p. 540) does not necessarily mean that all musical intervals can be reduced to integer ratios: presumably it would be possible for these ratios merely to function as convenient yardsticks for making whatever precise determinations of interval are musically necessary. While integer ratios do clearly play a disproportionate role in the formation of many musical styles, there is some evidence (confirmed by informal tests of my own) that the precise intervals preferred by musicians cluster round integer ratios rather than actually coinciding with them. Therefore to regard integer ratios as playing an intrinsically aesthetic role in these musical styles may well be to make a more deterministic association between psychological and musical categories than is warranted. There is of course no doubt that such associations are in order when simply seen as normative in this way - as in the case, for instance, of the association of conventional intervallic registration with the psychophysiology of pitch perception that has been proposed by Beament (<u>The Biology of Music</u>, p. 15).

Chapter 3:

Musical and psychological explanation

Introductory

When musicians imagine music they employ schematic models of musical sound: tokens which can be 'seen' or 'heard' in terms of the intended music, but which generally make little sense in themselves. In Chapter Four this interpretation of the everyday images of music - schemes in piano playing, performance scores and so forth - will be extended to the more elaborate, research models that we call musical analysis; but before going on to this there is a major objection to be met which has so far been ignored (apart from a brief outline in the Introduction). The starting point of my argument was the failure of analysts to describe the experience of music in a properly detailed and neutral manner - neutral in the sense that it would be possible to make valid generalizations about the aesthetic effect of music from the accounts of it offered by the analyst. The objection that could be raised is that it is not the modern analyst's intention to describe music in this sense at all. Indeed such analysts as Edward T. Cone and Hans Keller have specifically contrasted description and analysis. Both agree that description is essentially pointless because it merely duplicates what is obvious. By 'description' Cone means both the verbose programme note and the mechanical assignment of chordal or formal labels that requires no theoretical or critical judgement on the analyst's part.[1] Keller, according to whom "the age of description is over", makes the distinction between description and analysis by analogy with psychoanalysis. Freud (writes Keller) "demonstrated the unity of the most chaotically diverse dream by analyzing the <u>latent</u> content of the <u>manifest</u> dream"[2]: that is to say, he rendered the fragmentary and inconsequential contents of the conscious mind comprehensible by setting them in the context of the entire mind, unconscious as well as conscious. To analyze, therefore, is to get behind appearances: it is to show how the overt or obvious derives its significance and meaning from factors that are hidden. Echoes of Freud's thinking can be found in both Schoenberg and Schenker. Thus Schoenberg wrote that "the most remote overtones are recorded by the subconscious", suggesting that musical responses may be determined by factors of which the listener is not directly aware - much as Freud explained the behaviour of neurotics.[3] Again, Schenker talks of composers being "obsessed with the daemonic forces of the middleground and background", which has a Freudian ring; so does his statement that "the fundamental structure amounts to a sort of secret, hidden and unsuspected".[4] However, explaining the obvious in terms of the hidden is by no means the exclusive preserve of psychoanalysis. For example, to explain the perception of speech is not to describe how speech sounds to the listener but to derive his experience from psychological processes or formal structures of which he is unconscious. Economists, historians and scientists equally explain overt phenomena in terms of underlying, and often purely hypothetical, causation. So the topic of this chapter is not simply the analogy between musical analysis and psychoanalysis, but the broader concept of analysis as a more or less scientific type of explanation in which the particular properties of specific phenomena are derived from general underlying principles of a supposedly objective nature.

Such principles may be physical, psychological or cultural. An example of the explanation of music in terms of cultural symbolism at a fairly grandiose level is Levi-Strauss' analysis of Ravel's <u>Bolero</u>; its purpose is to show "the unconscious structuring of the work – patterns that have manifested themselves despite the avowed intentions of the composer".[5] Another example is the kind of social interpretation of music developed by Wilfred Mellers and refined to an amazing degree by John Shepherd, according to whom "the organization of musical structures is ultimately a dialectical correlate of the social reality that is symbolically mediated by and through the music of a particular society ... Pentatonicism and tonality have respectively mediated the mediaeval and industrial world senses".[6] What Shepherd is essentially saying is that music only reveals its full meaning when interpreted via the medium of the appropriate social and cultural symbolism. Does this mean that the ordinary listener is engaged in the same interpretative process, too? The answer to this would be, not necessarily; on the grounds that the significance revealed by such analysis is not necessarily aesthetic – for example, exotic music can have 'meaning' in the sense of helping to maintain an institutional order, without this function having any direct relationship to its specific aural properties; such 'meaning' would therefore be important to the social scientist but not the the western listener treating the music merely as a source of aesthetic pleasure.

How far Levi-Strauss, Mellers and Shepherd do in fact believe their explanations of music to be as unrelated as this to the process of aesthetic perception is sometimes hard to say; but when similar types of interpretation are practised at a level closer to the actual elements of musical style, it is obvious that the analysis is intended to say something about the process of perception as well as about the object of perception. For example, Cone has described the triad in classical tonality as a norm "with which all other [sonorities] are compared" (his purpose being to show how other musical formations can function similarly as norms in non-tonal styles). And here this comparison is meant as something the listener does as well as the analyst: thus Cone concludes that in music "there is always a normal to be found, and to be heard".[7] By discovering what this normal is (for example a particular tetradic segregation in Schoenberg's serial songs) the analyst reveals the significant form of a musical structure (in this case, the move from the tetradic segregation towards greater complexity, and final return to it, outlining an arch-like shape); so explaining what is happening when the listener reacts aesthetically to this form, even if the listener could not have consciously identified what it was that outlined that form. Cone's analysis is therefore intended as a psychological one, even if only by implication. By contrast, such psychological implications are explicitly worked out in Leonard Meyer's account of musical style, which is again based on the concept of the norm. According to Meyer "the customary or expected progressions of sounds can be considered as a norm ... and alteration in the expected progression can be considered as a deviation. Hence deviations can be regarded as emotional or affective stimuli".[8] Meyer's theory is based on the 'conflict theory of the emotions', according to which emotion results from the inhibition of a tendency to respond; so that the deviations which can be discovered through appropriate analysis of the musical score (analysis, that is, in terms of the correct norms) are to be understood as actual psychological determinants of the listener's emotional response. Thus Meyer explains the listener's conscious response to the music in terms of "expectations" and "deviations" of which he may well be unconscious ("unconscious expectation" therefore being defined purely in terms of the hypothesized psychological processes). Hence his analysis is intended to be at the same time musical and psychological, or more precisely it is to be justified as a musical analysis on the grounds that it is a correct psychological analysis.

Meyer's analysis of style, then, constitutes an attempt to discover the general principles that govern the formation of musical structures; principles deriving from nature or from the psychology of the individual, whose functioning is therefore in no way dependent upon the conscious awareness of them. Thus, speaking of the use of complex chords and timbre, Schoenberg wrote that "laws apparently prevail here. What they are, I do not know. Perhaps I shall know in a few years. Perhaps someone after me will find them. For the present all we can do is describe".[9] For Schoenberg, then, true explanation (as opposed to description) should be based on the discovery of natural laws, whether physical or psychological; and in his theoretical writings he was frequently at pains to distinguish such natural laws from the codified rules of the pedagogue with which he considered them to be often, and disastrously, confused.[10] Indeed one of the hallmarks of twentieth century analysis has been just such an attack on traditional pedagogical categories (conventional formal taxonomies, chord labelling and so forth) as being divorced from psychological, and hence musical, reality; Schenker went so far as to say that "all systems and scale formations which have been and are taught in the music and theories of various people were and are merely self-deception".[11] In this way the aim was to discover (rather than invent or merely codify) the real principles that govern music; and, because they are seen as determining the listener's response to music, such principles must either be themselves psychological, or - if capable of a purely formal statement - must at least have psychological consequences. However, though contemporary analysis invokes formal principles often enough, and derives aesthetically important properties of music from them, it is rarely spelled out precisely what these psychological consequences might be: explicit theories of the listening process are not offered. The following therefore is a reconstruction of the psychological implications of formal analysis in music, and concentrates on the most basic levels of musical perception since it is on these that any higher-level generalizations about aesthetically perceived structure must be based. The rest of the chapter will set out some of the problems that are created by maintaining such an account of musical listening.

Theories of unconscious psychological functioning implicit in modern analysis

Oswald Jonas pointed out[12] that it was frequently Schenker's practice to enunciate general principles of a psychological or even biological nature and then to derive specific musical practices from them: principles like "repetition ... is a biological law of life, physical as well as spiritual".[13]

Again, he wrote that "in nature sound is a vertical phenomenon" which "art horizontalizes" because "man ... within his own capacities can experience sound only in succession":[14] his technique of analysis therefore showed how, by means of prolongation through time, the natural properties of sound (as evident in the overtone series) were rendered perceptible as psychologically and musically meaningful forms.[15] However principles of this sort are undoubtedly obscure in that it is hard to see how they could be verified or refuted, and it is certainly fair to say that Schenker's works have been valued for the analytical insights they offer rather than for the theoretical principles on which these insights were supposedly based, and in terms of which they were expressed.

The hypothesis that music derives more or less directly from natural principles is however capable of more exact formulation and experimental treatment, such as Otto Szende attempted in a large series of tests into intervallic perception carried out in Hungary. The experiments involved pairs of tones which were played to subjects who had to judge whether they were too small, too large, or just right; the tests covered all the chromatic intervals. The intention was to evaluate how far purely psychological or biological factors, as opposed to cultural training, determined the intervallic categories of musical structures; and therefore the experiments were designed in such a way as to isolate the relevant mechanisms of intervallic perception from any extraneous factors. Hence only successive pairs of tones were used, in case acoustic beats between simultaneous tones should distort the results. And the tones were presented in an order specifically designed to neutralize any tendency listeners might have had to impute particular tonal contexts to the intervals.[16] Szende even avoided real orchestral sonorities for fear of irrelevant associations, arguing that "pitch discrimination can be and should be examined purely on the basis of the frequency given, and independently of timbre discrimination. The [sine] generator is, thus, an ideal source of sound".[17] The hypothesis being tested here is therefore that musical listening can be divided into a number of distinct functional mechanisms corresponding to the basic parameters of musical sound: one mechanism (the one under review) corresponding to pitch or interval discrimination, another presumably to timbre discrimination and so forth. If this hypothesis were correct, then it would be possible to generalize results obtained under such experimental circumstances to the real conditions of normal musical listening in the same way that scientific generalization is possible once underlying mechanisms have beeen isolated.

In fact the evidence would militate against the possibility of generalization from experiments like Szende's. It appears that the criteria by which intervallic judgements are normally made are largely absent from sine tones, especially at low intensities;[18] psychologically, therefore, pitch cannot be evaluated independently of timbre and dynamic level in the same sense that frequency can be isolated from waveform and intensity. It would therefore be surprising if Szende's experiments had isolated the functioning of a mechanism corresponding directly to the formation of musical intervals, and in fact Szende concluded that "musical hearing ... is a function of musical imagination, of 'tonal vision', which, in turn, is decisively influenced by aural training (musical education), musical practice, and the entire 'tonal world' of a particular society".[19] Such a conclusion is after all more or less inevitable if one is to account for the variation in musical style which is found in different cultures; if musical structures were directly determined by biological mechanisms, then the only way in which variations could be explained would be in terms of greater or lesser progress along the ladder of evolution. This in effect is how Schenker himself did see variations in musical style; he asserted that all primitive peoples would in time adopt the major scale.[20] His general condemnation of music since Brahms, too, follows directly from the fact that he saw the principles of musical formation with which his analytical method was concerned as being founded directly in human biology. The American analysts who since the last war have adopted and developed Schenker's techniques of hierarchical analysis naturally found such reactionary and ethnocentric beliefs highly uncongenial, and attempted to demonstrate that it was possible to apply the basic principles of Schenkerian analysis in a much more catholic manner than Schenker had himself allowed; mediaeval music, atonal music and Japanese music were all analyzed by Schenker-derived methods. Inevitably this meant abandoning Schenker's biological principles; and of the attempts to replace them with some other kind of theoretical underpinning, Benjamin Boretz' <u>Metavariations</u> was probably the most thoroughgoing.

Even Schenker had not in fact held that all aspects of music - for example, all intervals in use - could be derived exclusively from natural sound or biological principles: of the perfect fourth, and of the use of natural intervals related to tones other than the tonic, he wrote that "these notes are no longer actual overtones: they are only images of overtones ... It is therefore not permissable to ascribe the same significance to them".[21] Both Schoenberg and Schenker agreed that the minor mode was a purely artificial product, designed by analogy with the major mode, so that "attempts to represent it as something given in nature are pointless".[22] Both therefore saw musical structures as based on the perceptual properties of natural sound but elaborated culturally, so that different musical styles exploited these given properties in different ways. Now Boretz' theory of musical structure reversed this, in that he saw certain logical principles as shared between all possible musics, but their particular foundation in musical sound as culturally variable, being largely determined by convention or historical factors.[23] In <u>Metavariations</u> therefore he sketched what he called an "all-musical system" in which general properties of intervallic classes and so forth were presented formally by means of symbolic logic, along with the various logical relations possible between them (such as order determinacy, content determinacy, and so forth). Since the smallest units with which the system dealt, such as pitch or interval classes, were defined in terms of their relationship to larger syntactic structures, they were defined as units of significance rather than as sonic elements such as particular pitches or intervals: thus, for example, Boretz argued that an 'octave' should merely be defined as a modular unit of musical structure, rather than in terms of a specific acoustic realization (that is to say, a 2:1 frequency relationship).[24] By definition any formalization of music is predicated on the logical distinction between the significant structure and its particular sonic realization, so that according to Boretz "we need not <u>ever</u> construct sounds to construct music, regardless of their indispensibility for its transmission, for once we have exhausted their full burden of significant relational information ... we have no further <u>musical</u> use to put them to".[25] Naturally, there are general conditions regarding what sounds are capable of transmitting such musical content (they must not be excessively quiet, high and so on) but these are logically distinct from the musical structures and hence, in Milton Babbitt's words, "the discovery and formulation of these constraints fall into the province of the psycho-acoustician" rather than that of the music theorist or analyst.[26]

Now there is no intrinsic reason why a formal system of this sort should be regarded as having any implications for the psychology of music. It could be used as Boulez uses formal systems of his own invention, that is to say as a heuristic device consciously adopted by the composer. Or it could simply be regarded as a means of making precise statements about the musical score, without any implications as to the compositional process of the music, the listener's experience of it, or its aesthetic value. These would be entirely legitimate applications. However Boretz, like most formal analysts, does not restrict himself in such a way; and this means that substantial assertions, or at least hypotheses, about psychological functioning are involved in his applications of the system. Thus he uses it as an analytical technique for elucidating already existing music that was clearly not composed through the conscious use of any such calculi. He uses it as the basis for a number of historical and other deductions involving aesthetic value - perhaps composers abandoned freely atonal music in favour of serialism, he implies, because of the lack of hierarchical depth that becomes evident when it is analyzed formally.[27] Here, then, Boretz explains the aesthetic responses of composers or listeners - for that, presumably, is what was involved in the abandoning of one type of music in favour of another - not in terms of anything these composers or listeners would have been consciously aware of as such, but in terms of complex formal relationships which are only to be discovered by analysis. There is a close analogy here with language. Psycholinguists explain the perception of speech - and hence the possibility of responding to the meaning of what is being said - in terms of formal entities and relationships of which the listener is quite unaware, and which again can only be discovered through analysis. A theory, or at least a rationale, of unconscious process is thus implied, and this is equally the case of formal theories of music.

However, before going on to ask precisely what are the psychological implications of formal analysis in music, we should anticipate a possible source of confusion. Linguistic analysis is what the linguist does rather than what the listener does. In practice listeners do not discriminate each level of linguistic structure as it is described by the linguist. These structures represent the maximum linguistically significant information theoretically available in speech sound rather than the discriminations a listener will actually make on a given occasion. It is quite normal for people to hear things that are not actually present in the speech sound, or fail to hear things that are, because listening to someone talking is governed very largely by expectations regarding the meaning of what is being said. Much of the linguistic information theoretically available in speech sound is therefore redundant. Hence the linguist's analysis of speech is an abstraction of the identifications actually made in speech perception; it does not, or need not, directly represent the processes themselves.[28] The same argument can be applied to the formal analysis of music: it may not be appropriate to look for an immediate perceptual correlate to every formal structure or discrimination. For example, the derivation of a particular major or minor tonality from a more background level at which "the tonic" functions as a category of musical significance without differentiation of major or minor, which is part of Boretz' formal analysis of tonality,[29] may not directly represent a functional process in perception; Meyer has emphasized that the perception of serial music is not a direct function of its formal structure but is limited by psychological factors such as memory span.[30] Nevertheless Meyer does assume that the formal properties of musical structures are functionally related to the listener's aesthetic response, and this presupposes that such formal categories do represent, if not a literal description, then at least the rationale of the perceptual discriminations listeners actually make.

In determining exactly what the psychological implications of formal analysis are, as exemplified by Boretz, it is again helpful to refer to the study of speech perception as a guide. Empirical research into speech perception (phonetics) made little progress towards an understanding of how speech conveys linguistic meaning as long as it attempted to generalize merely from acoustic descriptions of speech sounds.[31] A systematic connection between speech sounds and semantic structure only became possible when researchers reversed the process by, first, analyzing language into its smallest units of meaning (phonemes) and then attempting to correlate these with speech sounds. Now, as the smallest unit of linguistic meaning, the phoneme is logically independent of the particular speech sounds by which it is communicated; it is not affected by sonic alterations such as vowel harmony and different tones of voice. However phonemes can be further analyzed into "distinctive features", which are not themselves units of meaning but elementary acoustic characteristics broad enough to be distinguishable in the normal variety of speech sounds. Specific combinations of these acoustic features serve to identify a given phoneme. The particular features used as the basis of linguistic communication vary from one linguistic community to another and their perception is clearly influenced by training; but the basic logical properties of their organization do not vary, and should therefore probably be regarded as psychologically or biologically determined. In this way psycholinguists analyzed the relationship between speech sound and linguistic meaning in terms of a hierarchical structure of signification by means of which purely cultural determinations of sound were linked with purely logical relationships of linguistic meaning.

It is not surprising, then, that the most comprehensive theory of musical perception along such lines is the work of a team of speech researchers: Paul Boomsliter and Warren Creel. Again the perceptual process is analyzed into a number of stages, connecting purely acoustic content at one end with purely formal relationships at the other. Boomsliter and Creel's theory is based on two considerations. The first is that pitch judgement is not a direct correlate to the funadamental frequency of a musical stimulus or even to the periodicity of an overall harmonic spectrum: rather it is a psychological construct, such that people discriminate pitches even when the periodicity of the musical stimulus is degraded, and their pitch judgements are affected by a number of contextually varying factors. The second is the privileged role, both in musical practice and in tests of pitch judgements, of groups of tones whose frequencies are related by low integer ratios. Putting these two considerations together, Boomsliter and Creel hypothesized that the discrimination of pitch involves two stages, the first of which constitutes an approximate judgement of pitch directly related to the periodicity of the musical stimulus, and the second of which is a precise judgement of pitch related to the particular melodic context of the music. As regards the latter, Boomsliter and Creel's suggestion was that successive intervals in a melody would be heard in terms of low-integer frequency ratios; this would cause the pitches actually experienced to drift in the course of a melody, so that for example the G on which the following phrase of the <u>Marseilleise</u> begins (Ex. 3.1) would be perceived as a slightly

Ex. 3.1

different G from that two bars later - multiplying out the ratios between successive tones, the octave betwen the two G's is given as 1:2.062.[32] Boomsliter and Creel proposed (and it is here that their theory becomes specifically musical as well as psychological) that this 'stretching' of the octave beyond the normal 2:1 ratio was responsible for the sense of tension and relaxation characteristic of melody; so that the conscious characteristics of the listener's experience - the ebb and flow of tension - could in this way be explained in terms of unconscious psychological processes, namely unconscious judgements of pitch and interval.

It is important to realize that beyond the initial, approximate coordination with stimulus periodicity, Boomsliter and Creel's theory is specifically concerned with psychological constructs. It is true that, in their view, vocal or violin performance of melodies - whose intonation is up to the performer rather than fixed - reflects these psychological factors (in fact they attempted to verify their theory by getting musicians to select intonations for given melodies by ear, and analyzing the results[33]); and under such circumstances there would be a direct correlation between the frequency of a tone (or at least the pitch that would be assigned to it in isolation) and the pitch it was perceived as having in a given melodic context. But the theory further implied that where melodies are played on fixed-intonation instruments like the piano, they will still be heard in terms of these contextual pitch constructs; and here it is obvious that the theory's mathematical analysis of the musical intervals refers to the psychological judgement of pitch and not to the physical attribute of frequency. In this way an extra stage, namely the judgement of pitch in given musical contexts, is interposed between frequency and musical response - as compared to Szende's attempt to correlate the two directly with each other and independently of musical context.

Now Boomsliter and Creel's account of the perception of musical intervals is considerably more complex than anything implied by Boretz, or for that matter by other formal analysts who discuss music exclusively in terms of equal-tempered semitones as the elementary units of significant structure. Since equal-tempered intervals do not vary with musical context - as do the intervals Boomsliter and Creel talk about - it is less immediately obvious that Boretz' theory is about psychological constructs rather than the physical attributes of the musical stimulus. Boretz however makes it clear that this is so: "a listener from an Eastern culture, learning that a given notation represented two attacks of the same pitch, might hear a Western-culturally 'correct' realization of that notation as an 'incorrect' succession of <u>two different pitches</u>, because his background pitch-structural vocabulary was more finely quantized than ours. For pitch-function assignments are <u>contextual</u>, and take place within thresholds that in practice enable such apparent anomalies as the assignment of discriminably different pitches to identical pitch functions, and of indiscriminable pitches to different pitch functions, depending on the <u>structural</u> context".[34] Such anomalies would clearly arise from the transformation between the elementary, and unconscious, judgement of pitch determined (as in the first stage of Boomsliter and Creel's theory) by the periodicity of the stimulus, and the second stage in which precise categorizations of pitch class are made in terms of the given musical and cultural context. Only such a multi-stage theory of pitch perception could plausibly account for the two facts, first, that attributions of pitch to isolated musical tones appear to be the same universally and are hence presumably determined by biological factors;[35] and secondly, that the perceptual categorizations of pitch class made in different musical cultures do vary and must therefore be influenced by training.

In this way the logical distinction between sound and

significant structure, on which formal analysis is predicated, is clearly made by analogy with the psychology of speech perception. And a further way in which this clarifies what is involved in the formal analysis of music is as regards what it purports to achieve. In either case to explain a particular configuration means to derive it from a more general level of significant structure – a level, that is, at which a function is defined though the particular formation that will fulfil this function is not. Although at the semantic level speech can be creative – that is to say, new meanings can be articulated through speech – at the level with which phonemic analysis deals it is deterministic: pre-established categories of linguistic structure are simply perceived correctly or incorrectly by the listener according to predefined rules of formation. Formal analysis of music sees music deterministically in formal terms; the listener either perceives the formal structure (whether consciously or unconsciously) or fails to perceive it. In fact, like phonemic analysis, formal musical analysis aims, so to speak, to delete the listener and to replace him by a theorem that correlates musical stimulus directly with cultural meaning by means of formal laws of signification. The most obvious manifestation of this is the repeated attempts to reduce the styles of pre-existing music – tonal music for example – to formal laws capable of being used for computer composition; but no less direct a consequence is the belief widespread in the last ten years or so that the good musical analysis is that which accounts for everything in a piece of music, and that an analysis which only accounts for a few aspects of it should be regarded as a half-way stage, a provisional step towards a total analysis.

To believe that music can, and should, be totally analyzed is simply the logical consequence of believing that musical analysis can be, and should be, founded upon psychologically valid categorizations: if we respond psychologically to a piece, the argument goes, then it must necessarily be possible to analyze that psychological response (and conversely, Boretz adds, if a piece cannot be analyzed successfully then what grounds can we have for caring for it?[36]) In this way recent American analysis can reasonably be seen as a direct attempt to fulfil Schoenberg's and Schenker's vision of an analytical method which would be psychologically true because based on psychologically functional categories and laws, and hence of a genuinely theoretical validity. There is no essential difference in intention between Schenker's attack on traditional formal categories or chord-labelling, and the American attempts to alter and redefine analytical terminology. The term 'chord', for example, became supplanted by 'simultaneity': the point being that 'simultaneity' is intended as a functional term defined in terms of precise syntactical relationships that could be unequivocally demonstrated, whereas 'chord' is an introspective term used loosely to refer to surface characteristics of musical presentation. There can thus never be explicit criteria as to whether a particular formation is a 'chord' proper or merely, say, the byproduct of a linear motion. In the same way Arthur Komar tried to define the precise structural conditions under which the term 'suspension' should be used; indeed Komar called "designing a set of rigorous term for music ... the serious but unfulfilled goal of current music theory".[37] The aim, then, was to overcome the subjectivity of normal descriptions of music by developing a terminology that had a theoretically determinable relationship, in the first place, to the score and, by implication, to the aesthetic significance of the music; and which would therefore bypass the individual listener's judgement with all its quirks and irrelevancies.

The score as a basis for analytical deduction

I

Since the aim of formal analysis is to make precise statements about objective data, the listener's response to music is more or less ignored. This is not because formal analysis is not intended to have any relationship to the listener's response — as we've seen, it is used as the basis for arguments about musical value — but simply because there is no way in which listeners' responses can be defined that is both objective and musically useful. It is possible to make scientific studies of the response to music on the basis of the words listeners apply to it, as in the various studies employing semantic differential technique;[38] or 'tonality' could be studied simply in terms of those situations in which listeners use the term 'tonal' or consider it appropriate. Alternatively scientific studies of musical response could be based on other types of observable behaviour, or by monitoring the listener's level of excitation by means of measurements of skin resistance and so forth. However such techniques invariably seem to produce criteria for musical identification which are too broad to be of any real use to the musical analyst, whose purpose is to make distinctions between one musical context and another at a considerably more detailed level.[39] Consequently formal analysts normally retain their objectivity by virtue of ignoring the listener's response and concentrating purely on the musical score as a statement of the data to be explained. When, for instance, Boretz analyzes the first eighteen bars of Brahms' Fourth Symphony in exhaustive detail,[40] all that is involved is the logical relations holding between the notational characters: the analysis is done 'blind', in the sense that the steps of the argument cannot be directly verified by aural judgement. The justification for this is that, as Boretz puts it, even an emotional reaction to music is a reaction to something determinate, and should therefore be capable of being elucidated by a precise analysis of that something.[41] The score is not <u>read</u> as a token of intended sound, in the sense in which (as we saw) performers and score-readers ordinarily read music; it is, so to speak, analyzed without ever being read. But a major assumption has clearly been made here, in that the score is taken as an adequate representation of the 'something determinate' to which listeners react; it is after all musical sound, not the score as such, that is being responded to in the concert hall. The principal question posed in this section is therefore how far notational categories (and in particular such categories as relate to pitch) constitute an appropriate basis for formal deductions concerning the aesthetic significance of the music to be drawn.[42]

When a formal analysis is made of, let us say, a string quartet, the score is treated as an objective representation of the musical structure - objective in the sense of being autonomous of a particular listener's reactions, or of the variations that normally occur between one performance and another. However the score is not objective in the sense that it has a theoretically determinable relationship to the physical sound produced by the four instruments. Over a series of hearings, and working from the sound alone, a trained listener can reconstitute the score of any but the most difficult quartet textures. But it would appear that aural dictation of this sort cannot be reduced to a precise series of theoretical operations carried out upon an objective representation of the musical sound: so that it is impossible to 'delete the listener' in defining the relationship between sound and score. To demonstrate this, let us consider trying to produce a computer transcription of a string quartet. The first stage is a mechanical conversion of the analogue signal into a series of digital values; a transformation which in theory degrades the physical sound by cutting out whatever happens on a finer scale than the sampling rate, but which in practice produces virtually no audible degradation of sound quality provided the sample rate is adequate. Problems arise, however, when it comes to programming the computer to analyze the sound into its component notes; at least if the input signal comes from a normal microphone (or set of microphones) registering the vibration of air in the concert hall - the vibrations, that is, that impinge upon the human listener's ears. The principal difficulty arises from room acoustics. The pattern of echoing and re-echoing normal in any concert acoustic is so complex that it would be virtually impossible to devise a program to reconstruct the signals emanating from the original sound sources - the instruments - from air vibrations in the auditorium; every microphone location in the auditorium (for example corresponding to each seat) would necessitate a separate program! But even if this were overcome, mathematical separation of the complex waveforms of string instruments would be far from straightforward (and in the case of instruments whose partials are inharmonic it is not obvious that it could be done at all). Even then, there would remain the difficulty of integrating the separated notes into the correct instrumental parts - for instance recognizing the G string of the violin as belonging to the same instrumental line as its D, A, and E strings though each of these has a quite individual timbre, and one moreover that varies from low to high position, with different styles of bowing and so forth.[43]

This idealized example already suggests the extent to which the normal human performance of hearing quartet sound as a set of distinct instrumental lines involves externally-imposed factors - the sight of the instrumentalists,[44] for example, or contextual considerations such as the logic of a harmonic progression, the expressive properties of a melodic line, or stylistic expectations. But suppose that we bypass all these factors by fitting all four instruments with metal strings throughout and using magnetic pickups located under each string as the signal source for computer analysis. The sound signal (or group of sound signals) now being analyzed constitute what is, in mathematical terms, a highly simplified model of the sound a human transcriber works from: and on this simplified basis the computer can be programmed to produce a score in which each instrumental line appears as a graph whose coordinates are on the one axis time, and on the other frequency (whether the latter is evaluated simply by tracking the fundamental frequency of the signal and ignoring partials, or by Fourier analysis or by other means does not matter for present purposes - under most circumstances each will produce the same results). But there still remain insurmountable problems in the transition between this frequency graph - which will show waverings due to vibrato, little glides and other such features which Carl Seashore dubbed 'sonance'[45] - and the discrete series of notes as which the conventional score represents musical sound. When slurred notes are joined by portamenti, where should the division between one note and the next be drawn? Within such notes, how should a single pitch be evaluated from the constantly changing values of vibrato? There are of course rules of thumb about the correlation of vibrato and overall pitch (it is normally said that the perceived pitch will correspond to the mean value of the vibrato range) but these are no more than rules of thumb since the basic research necessary to establish anything more has never been done.[46] Furthermore it is entirely likely that the perceived pitch is not merely a direct function of the stimulus, but is also affected by the musical context. This, at any rate, is clearly true of the categorization of discrete pitch into musical pitch class that would constitute the final stage of such a computer transcription. Thus the simplest way to program the transformation of pitch into pitch class would be a literal assimilation to the nearest equal-tempered category. Such a transformation, taking no regard of the particular musical context, would however produce incorrect results: Victor Zuckerkandl[47] cites tests in which, in given musical contexts, listeners have accepted as correct intonation deviations of well over fifty cents from notated pitch values - so that for instance a frequency that in isolation would be judged nearer D will, in particular contexts, be heard as a C# (and would be so notated in a musician's transcription of the sound).

Clearly, then, a musical score cannot be considered objective in the sense of having any strictly determinable relationship to the physical sound of music; so much is indeed implied by Boretz' description of "anomalies" of this sort. However it is equally clear that it cannot be considered objective in the sense of specifying the psychological judgements of pitch listeners make in given contexts - in the way that Boomsliter and Creel's theory of intervallic perception attempts to do explicitly, and as Boretz' system does by implication. The difficulty is that, however they are interpreted, the categorizations of pitch built into conventional performance scores are much less contextually sensitive than are listeners' judgements or indeed actual performance. It has been repeatedly shown (and not only by Boomsliter and Creel but by Seashore's team and Charles Shackford among others[48]) that the intervals judged correct in particular contexts by listeners and performers correspond neither to equal temperament nor to other fixed intonations such as Pythagorean or Just; nor even to the slight degree of contextual variation introduced by enharmonic notation. At the same time, it is clear that such variations as occur are by no means a matter of indifference; good intonation is one of the principal qualities of good violin performance, and one to which even untrained listeners seem to be quite sensitive (even if they cannot attribute the clean and incisive sound that results to intonation as such). Consequently, regarded as a representation of judgements of pitch made in particular contexts, notational categories constitute no more than an approximate guide which misrepresents or omits information crucial for the effect the music makes on the listener. Information is omitted, of course, not only in the domain of pitch but also, and indeed to a greater extent, in other parameters of musical sound. To perform detailed, deductive analysis upon categories representing the actual values of musical pitches and other musical parameters in so approximate a manner, therefore, must result in analytical models owing more to the formal conventions of notation than to either the physical or the psychological properties of the music in question. Because there is only an imprecise relationship between the score-based analysis (which is precise in its own terms) and those properties of the musical sound to which the listener responds, formal analysis characteristically blends precision and imprecision in a curious way: aurally obvious harmonic or melodic motions are, so to speak, projected obliquely onto notational categories so that they become visible in the analytical reduction only in a distorted or incomplete manner; little systems appear which 'explain' a bar or two in terms of some underlying theorem, only to peter out for no apparent reason. As I said in Chapter Two, it is like trying to make sense of an embroidered fabric by looking at great detail at the back of it while ignoring the front.

II

Notated pitch relationships however do not only show less than is musically important (in approximating the pitch values actually employed and responded to); they also show more than is musically important, in the sense that scores represent as pitch musical events which may not be perceived in terms of discrete pitches at all. We saw that the precise relationship between frequency and musical pitch in a given context could be determined not by means of an immediate correlation but only through some sort of contextual analysis in terms of pitch relationships intuitively judged 'right' by a listener or a performer: in this sense the only precise criterion of a pitch relationship in music is this experienced feeling of 'rightness' or 'sweetness' or 'depth of sonority' that it elicits – or perhaps the sense of tensional direction that Boomsliter and Creel spoke of. But much of the texture of, for instance, Strauss' <u>Elektra</u> is not heard in any such way. Thus in passages of rapid vocal declamation some of the singers' notes are likely to have virtually no perceptible pitch at all, the vocal sonorities at most being kept 'in place' in terms of pitch by the accompaniment; again, there are frequently clusters of instrumental tones that are heard percussively, and in which therefore any distinct perception of pitch seems wholly lacking.

It seems doubtful that this can be, as the analogy with speech perception might suggest, simply a question of precise pitch relationships being perceived unconsciously but not registered consciously as such by virtue of the speed or complexity of the music. After all, when students write down complex chords in aural training – where several listenings are allowed over a much longer period than is available in the concert hall – the difficulty lies not merely in deciding what the relations between the perceived pitches are, but equally in hearing the chord as a complex of distinct pitches in the first place. However, some such process as this seems to be predicated by formal analyses of musical scores, based as they are upon the logical distinction of sound and significant structure. Through his deliberate identifications of the pitches making up a complex chord, the aural trainee transforms what is initially an immediately aural response - <u>this</u> sound - into a response which is logically independent of sound (a structure, that is, representable by means of conventional notation, or as a set of numbers, or in terms of locations on the keyboard). In this way it is possible to perceive music in terms of structures logically independent of sound, but this can often be done only by virtue of special training and an effort which either is conscious or, if not, is unconscious only in the way that any skilled activity can become so. As I said in Chapter One, perceiving music this way is not part of normal musical listening, but a quite separate and independent type of listening that can be brought to bear upon the musical sound; a type of listening, in fact, that is largely incompatible with normal aesthetic enjoyment.

By contrast, the transformation of purely sonic qualities into semantic categories logically independent of sound is - at least in principle - a necessary stage in the normal perception of speech. As I said, speech perception involves a hierarchical structure of significations whose highest level is the conscious experiencing of linguistic meaning; and underlying which are identifications, such as that of phonemes, which are not only unconscious but autonomic (meaning that they cannot be rendered conscious even through a special effort). If one speaks of the perception of phonemes, therefore, 'perception' refers not to a conscious judgement but to an unconscious process whose logical necessity is demonstrated by linguistic analysis: as Roman Jakobson puts it, "the phoneme functions, ergo it exists!"[49] In this way the interface between sonic medium and formal structure, on which any formal analysis is predicated, occurs at quite different levels in the cases of speech perception and of musical perception; and a consequence of this is that it is considerably less clear quite what sense it makes to speak in terms of the 'unconscious perception' of pitch relationships, in the way that it does in the case of phonemes. If to perceive a precise pitch relationship is actually to experience it in a certain way, then there is something obscure about the attempt to explain the listener's conscious experience of music in terms of unconsciously perceived pitch structures.

If this argument is correct, then those notes in a musical score such as <u>Elektra</u> which are not consciously experienced as having any precisely determinable pitch are functioning musically in a quite different manner from those that are. They might be heard as distinct pitches in aural training; they may have to be 'pitched' by the instrumentalist during performance; but as far as the ordinary listener is concerned they have no immediate psychological denotation as discrete pitches. They simply represent, in a rather indirect manner, some of the stimulus properties of the music, or (more immediately) directions to the performer which when executed have certain effects upon the listener's experience which are not however specified by the score.[50]

To analyze the score deductively, then, is not only to magnify the imprecisions of notational pitch categories, but to treat as having an intrinsic significance some categories that have no direct relationship to experienced sound at all. Nor is this criticism to be restricted to the extreme versions of formal analysis current in America. It is just as applicable to Schoenberg's definition of tonality (quoted in Chapter One) as the art of combining tones such that "the relation of all events to a fundamental tone is possible": for it is only in terms of notational categories that an explicit relationship can be established between all the pitches in a composition and its overall tonal centre. Except at a fairly localized scale such explicit relationships will not often be consciously perceived by most listeners. Sometimes they will nevertheless have an indirect effect of some sort upon the listener's experience; it is possible to feel a certain sense of distance or loss in a modulation at a tritone, without having perceived that relationship in terms of precise tonal organization, or even knowing that it was a modulation that was responsible for the effect. Often however large-scale relationships will have no perceptual consequences for listeners; meaning, not that they are perceived unconsciously, but simply that they are not perceived. So the relating of all the events to the tonic which Schoenberg speaks of is primarily something that the analyst does and not the listener. This, as we saw, was also true of the formal relationships involved in phonemic analysis. But there is an essential difference as between the two cases. The formal relationships the phonemic analyst talks about do at least represent a functional rationale of perceptual judgements that ordinary listeners do make unconsciously; if they were not functional in this sense, the psycholinguist would have no justification for talking about them. But the formal relationships the musical analyst talks about may bear no relationship to the ordinary listener's judgements, conscious or unconscious. If the musical analyst is justified in talking about them, then, it is not because he is in the first instance talking about the ordinary listener's perception of the music, but because (as I suggested in Chapter

One) he is talking about a quite different way of perceiving it. To use our recurrent image: he is talking about the back of the musical fabric.

III

The score of a piece of music, then, is in no sense a direct representation of its musical sound but rather combines certain characteristics of the musical stimulus with those of the listener's response, and combines them in a quite informal manner. Furthermore there is another respect in which what the score represents is neither the musical stimulus nor the listener's response as such, but certain aspects in which each remains invariant as between different performances of the score; it represents, in other words, 'the piece' as an abstraction from any given performance. Now such abstraction is again quite informal, in the sense that the relationship between 'the piece' and any given interpretation of it is not objectively definable. Speaking of the variants of Barbara Allen, Charles Seeger wrote that "no such entity as 'the Barbara Allen tune' can be set up other than for temporary convenience ... the very notion 'when [it] began to be itself' is metaphysical".[51] Instead the relationship between 'piece' and performance is an ad hoc one, in which aesthetic values are involved; hence it varies from one musical style or culture to another. The most detailed orchestral score, for instance one of Richard Strauss', represents the composition as an invariant between different performances: performances in which interpretation, certain aspects of orchestral sonority (for example French as against English woodwinds), and hall acoustic will differ. In baroque scores the degree of permissible variation (in instrumentation, ornamentation and so forth) is of course much greater. In oral traditions of music it may indeed be impossible to define 'the piece' as a determinate temporal extension at all; the repertoire of the African Pygmies, for example, is classified into set pieces by native musicians, but these pieces can only be defined in terms of a collection of melodic or harmonic formulae quite indirectly related to the sound of any particular performance[52] (the same applies, of course, to some indeterminate music of the post-war period).

Thus to a greater or lesser degree any composition (except an electronic one) is, so to speak, a 'theme' of which different performances constitute 'variations'; and here there is an important difference between the situation of the normal listener and that of the musical analyst. Essentially the listener responds not to 'the piece' as an abstraction but to the particular noise it makes on a certain occasion. The distinction is not, of course, a hard and fast one; any listener awaits a performance of a Beethoven symphony with a certain set of expectations to which the performance will be referred: nevertheless when the performance begins these expectations largely recede into the background as the sound of the particular performance engulfs the listener and absorbs his attention. The score, as denoting 'the piece' solely as an invariant between performances, therefore relates only at a remove to the listener's interest in the music; whereas it relates considerably more directly to the analyst's interests. For to analyze music, as it is generally understood and practised, is not to focus upon the properties of the individual performance, but upon precisely those aspects of musical design which, by and large, remain invariant between one performance and another. Similarly the analyst is, to a much greater degree than the average listener, interested in aspects of musical design on the large scale; whereas (as we saw in Chapter One) such large-scale aspects of musical structure can be related only quite loosely to the listener's experience, the score makes them clear.

The contradiction of formalistic analysis of music, then, is that it adopts rigorous scientific methods of deduction while applying them to a representation of the music - the score - which is not remotely objective in the sense that scientific data need to be if strict deductions from them are to be of value.[53] The score predicates specific cultural values; it is made up of symbols whose precise denotation is left undefined and has to be determined within the particular musical context; it has in short to be <u>read</u> as music, if it is to make sense as music. On the other hand to base an analysis on a more genuinely objective representation of musical sound, while justifiable as a scientific procedure, more or less precludes illuminating conclusions about musical design, since such design frequently has little direct relationship to the objective structure of the musical stimulus. A digital representation of musical sound, such as we discussed in the string quartet example or such as is employed in the recording industry, obviously contains the information an analyst needs to make illuminating observations about large scale design; but the only way to get at this information is to synthesize the digital representation and listen to the result (as in a modern digital recording). The digital score has, in short, to be <u>heard</u> as music if it is to make sense as music. To 'delete the listener' is to cease talking about music at all.

In general, then, it seems reasonable to say that the analyst (and this includes the formal analyst) is only tangentially interested in things that either have, or can be derived directly from, physical or psychological reality. Because his terminology for music is not wholly objective but also aesthetic, in that its precise denotations vary with the particular musical context, the analyst can hardly formulate objective theories of psychological functioning – theories, for example, regarding the absolute duration of experienced tonal centricity under conditions of modulation, or of the perceptual categorization of musical textures into figure and ground. He is not, in other words, concerned with precise, autonomous structures of signification which can be abstracted from a sonorous, aesthetic and indeed emotional context, in the way that linguistic structures can. Hence music theory and linguistics do not have the same kind of relationship to psychological studies of perception. The formal linguist's studies are pursued more or less independently of the experimental psychoacoustician's but between the two disciplines there is an explicit, if idealized, theory of functional inter-relation. In essence the linguist is as much a scientist as the psychoacoustician; the two scientific disciplines are related to each other in much the same way as, for example, engineering is based on materials sciences. By contrast, the musical analyst has an altogether different kind of interest in musical sound from that the psychoacoustician has; the analyst may work on the back of the fabric of musical sound, but he is still interested in it as music rather than simply as sound. His motives may not be immediately aesthetic, but he works within an aesthetic context.

Notes

1: *Analysis Today*, p. 34-5. See also Meyer, *Explaining Music*, p. 9.

2: *The Chamber Music*, p. 91.

3: These ideas received their fullest treatment in Ehrenzweig's *Psychoanalysis of Artistic Vision and Hearing*.

4: *Free Composition*, p. 111, 9.

5: Hopkins, *The Homology of Music and Myth*, p. 254.

6: *Whose Music?*, p. 84.

7: *Sound and Syntax: an introduction to Schoenberg's Harmony*, p. 22, 40.

8: *Emotion and Meaning in Music*, p. 32.

9: *Theory of Harmony*, p. 421.

10: Ibid, p. 8 ff.

11: *Free Composition*, p. 162.

12: Schenker, *Harmony*, p. 11 n. 8.

13: *Free Composition*, p. 118. Schenker several times refers to the "biological characteristics of tones" in *Harmony*, thus p. xxv, 84.

14: *Free Composition*, p. 10, 14.

15: This was of course a common theory at the time, shared for instance by Schoenberg (*Theory of Harmony*, p. 28).

16: <u>Intervallic Hearing</u>, p. 36.

17: Ibid, p. 42-4.

18: Benade, <u>Fundamentals of Musical Acoustics</u>, p. 287.

19: <u>Intervallic Hearing</u>, p. 158.

20: <u>Harmony</u>, p. 53-4.

21: <u>Free Composition</u>, p. 12.

22: <u>Theory of Harmony</u>, p. 94.

23: This is the same position as is argued by D.L. Harwood (<u>Universals in Music</u>, p. 527 ff); Harwood sees this as a direct consequence of perceptual and cognitive processes, and makes the same analogy with speech perception as I argue is implied by Boretz' theory.

24: <u>Metavariations</u>, PNM 1971, p. 257.

25: <u>Metavariations</u>, PNM Spring/Summer 1970, p. 63.

26: <u>Past and Present Concepts of the Nature and Limits of Music</u>, p. 9.

27: <u>Metavariations</u>, PNM Spring/Summer 1973, p. 177-8. Zuckerkandl in effect makes a similar identification of aesthetic value with hierarchical depth in terms of traditional Schenkerian analysis (<u>Man the Musician</u>, p. 206 ff). Cone even condemned Schoenberg's early songs on the grounds of the lack of hierarchical isomorphism they display as between sound, succession and syntax - terms which can only be defined by means of formal theory (<u>Sound and Syntax: an Introduction to Schoenberg's Harmony</u>, p. 24 ff). This is essentially the same aesthetic argument that Boulez used against Schoenberg's rhythms.

28: On this issue see Jakobson and Waugh, <u>The Sound Shape of Language</u>, p. 33; Neisser, <u>Cognitive Psychology</u>, p. 183 ff; Herriott; <u>Attributes of Memory</u>, p. 67.

29: <u>Metavariations</u>, PNM 1971, p. 238.

30: <u>Music, the Arts, and Ideas</u>, p. 276 ff.

31: Jakobson, <u>Six Lectures on Sound and Meaning</u>, p. 18 ff.

Creel, Boomsliter and Powers specifically refer to this as a methodological principle in <u>Tone Sensations as Perceptual Forms</u>, p. 534.

32: <u>Extended Reference</u>, p. 18-19.

33: These tests must be regarded as inconclusive, mainly because of the design of the 'search organ' on which they were conducted. This was an organ with an extended range of intervals, the keys for which were arranged in bands corresponding to integer ratios. Apart from delimiting the choices of intonation available, the visual analogue of the intonation provided by the keyboard must inevitably have meant that theoretical preconceptions affected the subjects' performance. Preliminary tests I have done, using a computer synthesis programme which overcomes these and certain other objections, does appear to confirm that there are consistent shifts of intonation dependent on musical context; but the intonations chosen by no means wholly coincide with the integer ratios Boomsliter and Creel assume to be decisive.

34: <u>Nelson Goodman's Languages of Art</u>, p. 35.

35: Harwood, <u>Universals in Music</u>, p. 525.

36: <u>Metavariations</u>, PNM Spring/Summer 1973, p. 189.

37: <u>Theory of Suspensions</u>, p. 11.

38: For instance Plomp, <u>Aspects of Tone Sensation</u>; Faltin, <u>Phänomenologie der Musikalischen Form</u>.

39: Thus for example see Harrer and Harrer, <u>Music, Emotion and Autonomic Function</u>.

40: <u>Metavariations</u>, PNM Fall/Winter 1969, p. 71.

41: <u>Metavariations</u>, PNM Spring/Summer 1973, p. 160 ff.

42: A brief attack on the deductive analyses of scores was made by Martin, <u>Modes of Explanation in Analytical Discourse</u>, p. 180-4.

43: Risset, <u>Musical Acoustics</u>, p. 544.

44: Davies, <u>Psychology of Music</u>, p. 40.

45: Seashore, Psychology of Music, p. 103 ff.

46: See Ward, Musical Perception, p. 423. Charles Seeger discusses the mutual dependence of vibrato and tempo rubato in Studies in Musicology 1935-75, p. 177.

47: Sound and Symbol, p. 79-80.

48: A convenient summary with references is to be found in Ward, Musical Perception, p. 414-22.

49: Six Lectures on Sound and Meaning, p. 69.

50: Here there are undoubtedly genuine issues regarding the relationships between musical experience and unconscious perceptual processes. Just what levels of synthesis are involved in different musical textures, how far are they subject to the listener's voluntary control, how far are they determined by structural considerations (harmonic progression, for instance) as against immediate physical or psychological factors such as acoustic beats? Such psychological issues underlie the experience of musical texture described in Chapter 1, and might for instance be brought to bear upon the definition of line offered by Scruton (pp. 42, 63 above): thus it is quite possible that the precise psychological values of intonation discussed earlier are tied up with the perception of musical lines as such. At the level of fine intonation several characteristics of unconscious perceptual construction are evident: for instance, the perception of a musical note as having a particular quality of intonation is in general involuntary, much as is the perception of speech sound in terms of phonemic categories, and in both cases the judgements involved are more or less irreversible (that is, if either is for some reason heard 'wrong', it is virtually impossible to 'think back' to the raw sound and reinterpret it); both are to a large degree dependent on context rather than stimulus properties; and alterations in intonation may not be experienced as such but rather as changes in some other parameter such as timbre (Boomsliter and Creel, Research Potentials in the Auditory Characteristics of Violin Tone, p. 1991). All these attributes suggest that the perception of fine intonation involves unconscious interpretation, in contrast to the conscious level of pitch identification according to notational or analytical categories that is carried out in aural training and in which such attributes are either not found or found only to a lesser degree. However such issues of unconscious perception could only be properly studied by means of experimentation, and not through introspection or conventional musical analysis based on scores.

51: Studies in Musicology 1935-75, p. 312.

52: The Use of Playback Techniques in the Study of Aural Polyphonies, p. 483.

53: Thus semiotic analysis as practised by Nattiez is predicated on the doubtful premise that there can be derived from the score, by means of strict parsing techniques, "a neutral and immanent description of the object". This is intended to be independent of (and so to make possible a scientific analysis of) what he calls the "esthetic" and "poietic" poles of the music (The Contribution of Musical Semiotics to the Semiotic Discussion in General, p. 136).

Chapter Four:

A rationale of analytical practice

Analytical argument and its value

Musical scores do not, then, furnish an adequate basis of making firm deductions about the psychological functions that underlie the listener's response to music. Nevertheless there are instances when deductions made from musical scores can have an obvious validity. These princicipally occur when the music has been constructed in terms of an explicit formal logic, so that the design can be 'seen' without any aesthetic response to musical sound being necessarily involved. Sometimes an extramusical 'message' is built into the music, which can be reconstructed more or less mechanically once the code is known; secret names as in Schumann and Berg are a well-known example of this, and Wilfred Mellers' interpretations of Stravinsky's Oedipus Rex and Symphony of Psalms in terms of key symbolism[1] should probably be seen this way too. Hidden 'messages' of this sort merge, however, into hidden designs of a more formal nature, which again can be reconstructed mechanically once the code is found. For example, Stockhausen's Gruppen is designed in terms of rhythmic levels - 'formants', as Stockhausen himself called them. To reconstruct this design it is merely necessary to rearrange the orchestral score so that the rhythmic levels are set in order one above the other - tones held for whole bars at the bottom, then divisions of the bar into two, three, four equal beats and so on. When this is done, it becomes easy to see how the music is laid out in groups of 'formants', the presence or absence of rhythmic levels delineating shapes of some decorative merit.[2] An analysis of this sort is done purely in terms of notational symbols: the aural properties of the music, and hence the listener's response to it, are not directly involved. Indeed there are instances where this kind of reconstruction of formal design requires the aural properties of the music to be contradicted.

An interesting example of this is Skryabin's Fifth Sonata. The first question in analyzing this single-movement sonata is likely to be: what key is it in? That the question is relevant to an understanding of the formal structure, in a way it is not in the Seventh Sonata, is suggested both by the employment of key-signatures and by the use of modulatory relationships in defining the overall form. Nevertheless the answer to the question is not immediately obvious, partly because Skryabin's harmonies are highly chromatic but more particularly because they are almost invariably heard as dominants or dominant substitutes of tonics that are themselves less well defined. Purely aural considerations are very indecisive as regards the opening (Ex. 4.1), which is

Ex. 4.1: Skryabin, Fifth Sonata, opening

heard more as a shadowy emergence from tonal obscurity (in the manner, for example, of Tchaikowsky's <u>Francesca da Rimini</u>

or Liszt's B minor Sonata) than as a definite statement of tonal direction. The first main subject, however, is heard as a reasonably unmistakable, if somewhat pandiatonic, B major (bar 47, Ex. 4.2). To make this fairly immediate aural

Ex. 4.2: Skryabin, Fifth Sonata, first subject

judgement, however, is to make the large-scale tonal design of the sonata incomprehensible. Thus the B major produces an odd (though not of course impossible) relationship with the second subject area (bar 119) which is in an explicit B^b major; more importantly it fails to connect with the final section of the work which is in an equally explicit E^b major (as witness all the tonic pedals from bar 388 to the end). Moreover the B major is contradicted by Skryabin's key-signature, which is that of F# major or D# minor rather than B major. The evidence of the key-signature, in fact, suggests that the sonata should be seen as being in D# minor (or E^b minor). This means that there is now a conventional dominant relationship between first and second subject areas. Since the thematic recapitulation at bar 329 is in what we now see as A^b minor, the transposition of the entire passage including the modulation at a fifth results in the E^b major of the tonal recapitulation. Overall, then, this interpretation of the work reveals a staggering of thematic and tonal form enclosed within a tonic minor-major relationship; the same formal structure, in fact, as is found in the first movements of Chopin's B^b minor Sonata and of Tchaikowsky's Pathétique Symphony - both works which Skryabin would presumably have known well. Furthermore, such an interpretation clarifies the tonal inflection of the introduction to Skryabin's sonata as an essentially Neapolitan area superimposed upon a tonic pedal.

Here, then, the tonal design emerges precisely when the immediate aural properties of the first subject are set aside; if my account is accepted then it is possible to say that this subject 'sounds' as if it were in B major but 'is really' in D# minor. The 'reality' referred to in this formulation is not therefore defined by sound or determinable by aural judgement; in essence it is historical. Now analytical deductions of this sort are in general made, and justified, probabilistically: it cannot be proved from musical evidence alone that such design, or even the near-serial structure of the Seventh Sonata, is not fortuitous; it is merely that it is not very likely. Nevertheless such an analytical interpretation could be refuted by historical evidence, in the unlikely event of its becoming available; if an autograph were discovered labelled 'Sonata in B major', then no plausible sense would remain in which the sonata could still be regarded as 'really' in D# minor. In the same way all the examples of deductive analysis so far discussed in this chapter - that is, the examples of Schumann, Berg, Stravinsky, Stockhausen and Skryabin - are essentially assertions of historical fact which could in principle be verified or refuted by historical evidence.

In this way deductions made on the basis of the score are perfectly legitimate providing no claim is made that they have any direct or privileged reference to the psychological or aesthetic properties of the music; under such conditions we know what we are talking about. The majority of analysis, however, does not restrict itself in such a way. Rather it combines formal argument with specific assertions about the aural or aesthetic experience of the music, and here we may sometimes find ourselves unclear exactly what it is we are talking about – even when we have no doubt that the analysis is in fact of value. To some extent, of course, this was illustrated by the kind of aesthetic deductions Boretz made, and which were discussed in the last chapter; but the trouble with American formal analysts is that they rarely do talk in much detail about the aural experience of the music under analysis, and this point is therefore better illustrated by analytical methods which attempt to combine close attention to aural experience with formal arguments about the musical structure. A case in point is the kind of motivic analysis developed by Schoenberg and his followers, in which aural description and formal argument are inter-related by means of a complex and explicit theory of psychological function.

The term 'motive' is sometimes used to refer to a musical structure and sometimes to denote some kind of psychological process. Thus it can be used as a more or less straightforward description of musical texture: in this sense it is a fact, for instance, that Richard Strauss' music generally works motivically while Schubert's does not. However as used by Reti, Keller or Alan Walker, the concept of the musical 'motive' is intended as more than a mere technical description. Their motivic analyses are in effect assertions about the compositional process, in which objective properties of the musical score are explained in terms of such general psychological hypotheses as the timeless nature of the unconscious mind.[3] The basic principle of such motivic analysis is that all musical form is a diversification of an initial 'motive' or 'idea' that is experienced independently of temporal extension. To discover a certain motivic shape at different levels of formal structure - in a tiny fragment of figuration, or extended over the largest formal scale - is seen as retracing this process of compositional diversification. Hence the musical 'idea' primarily denotes a psychological entity that exists in the unconscious mind; only contingently is it to be identified with the 'motivic' texture characteristic of Strauss' music but not Schubert's. However the theory is that this process of diversification from the basic 'idea' is not only fundamental to all musical composition, but an essential criterion of musical value; the formal design of a composition is experienced as aesthetically good precisely to the extent that it follows inevitably from the underlying idea. Consequently, the argument goes, in all great music it must be possible, at least in principle, to discover a basic idea that is diversified; and it is the analyst's job to do just this. Used in this way, then, the terms 'idea' and 'motive' refer simultaneously to the formal properties of the music and the psychological properties of the experience.

But how is the theory to be applied in any particular instance? According to Keller it is merely a matter of listening: thus he describes his method as "essentially naive", explaining that "by this I mean that I listen inwardly to contrasts until their unity emerges, and without any theoretical preconceptions".[4] This may be simple enough where the music happens to work motivically in the descriptive sense; but when it does not, it is far from clear how judgements as to what it is that is being diversified can be made in purely aural terms. Consider for example an attempt to identify the underlying idea of the third of Schoenberg's Six Little Piano Pieces Op. 19. Given the outward diversity of its sonorities, can we discover some characteristic property which is common to them, and which is fundamental to our aesthetic response to the music? For example, we might suppose that its basic idea has to do with its characteristic harmonic formations, such as the major seventh enclosing major or minor thirds, which is responsible for the rather clenched tonal sonority that is characteristic of this piece; tendencies towards harmonic motion are neutralized within each chord, so that tensions build up which are not resolved. On the other hand, much the same harmonic vocabulary is equally characteristic of the other pieces of the set, and indeed of the Op. 11 piano pieces too; so that if there is some musical property which characterizes Op. 19/3 in particular, it is not simply harmonic vocabulary. Nor can it be the harmonic progressions as such, since it is hardly possible to devise a harmonic reduction of the piece which retains the characteristic qualities of the music while omitting its particular linear formations. Yet it is hardly possible to maintain that the basic idea of the piece lies in its specific linear formations to the exclusion of its other structural characteristics, because it is not hard to concoct a number of recognizably different pieces from more or less the same linear formations; and if some of these remain fairly close to the original as regards sonority and expression, others do not (Ex. 4.3).

Ex. 4.3: Two variants of Schoenberg's Op. 19/3

For the listener, such a series of purely aural judgements as these may serve to throw into relief the characteristic properties of the piece as it is experienced. By listening to the music in this active, experimental way one does indeed develop a kind of 'idea' of the music, a kind of timeless image that combines a certain sense of its formal attributes - the quasi-spatial disposition into balancing phrases, for instance - with qualities that are purely sonorous and expressive. And it is not hard to believe that Schoenberg might have begun with just such an 'idea'. But this subjective kind of 'idea' seems to have no immediate correlate in any particular aspect of the formal structure visible in the score, so that we have not succeeded in analyzing the music in the sense of making an explicit and demonstrable connection between aesthetic experience and formal evolution. We have in other words failed to establish a theory of musical functioning. It would appear, then, that when something more than a simple textural description is intended by the terms 'motive' and 'musical idea', something more than a simple aural judgement is required to define what is meant by it. And indeed motivic analyses do in practice contain a considerable amount of deduction, in the sense that intervallic patterns are discovered and followed through which, at first glance, were by no means obvious; you may not have been consciously aware of it, the analyst is saying, but here you can see what the basic idea is. And again, following one of these motivic tables through the music can indeed sharpen the listener's perception of it, persuading him to 'hear' connections where otherwise he did not, or throwing local details into a larger perspective. At the same time music is so richly detailed a stimulus that these tables are undoubtedly unconvincing considered simply as strict deductions from the score;[5] other motives can always be found (except perhaps in the case of descriptively 'motivic' music like Strauss') that are equally valid as strict deductions from the score, even though they may be entirely unconvincing from the musical point of view. So when we accept one motivic analysis as right, and reject another, we do not do this on the basis of its correctness in purely formal terms. Nor is it because its validity can be explained by means of any external criteria. The psychological processes asserted to go on in the composer's (or listener's) mind cannot be directly demonstrated: we do not ask, where in the brain should we look for the musical idea, and with what instruments are we most likely to detect it? Nor will historical evidence suffice to establish a motivic identification. If the composer says that his first idea for a piece consisted of some effect of orchestration – which was perhaps modified or even abandoned in the course of composition anyhow – then the motivic analyst may well say: that wasn't the real 'idea', but merely what happened to trigger off the external process of composition. And if a particular analytical interpretation cannot be refuted by historical evidence, it can hardly be established by it either.

In this way motivic analysis presents us with a dilemma. On the one hand, listening to music in the questioning way Keller describes, or following some little pattern of notes through the musical texture, can be of a musical value which is intuitively clear enough: that is not in doubt. On the other hand, the underlying idea of unconscious diversification seems incapable of being established as certain, or even probable, whether by means of an aural judgement or formal deduction. Indeed if in the course of a motivic analysis we ask ourselves: what are we talking about? a pattern of notes? an aural experience? something believed to go on in the unconscious mind? something that happened in the course of composition? - then we may well find ourselves at a loss for an answer; though intuitively we may know well enough that we are talking about something. Nor is this a problem restricted to motivic analysis. Schenkerian analysis for instance leans as heavily as does that of Schoenberg's followers on the assumption that there exist musical ideas which are at the same time aesthetically decisive, and capable of being defined independently of immediate aural experience. Thus Schenker seems to have seen the principles of voice-leading as referring to the mental forms of music's conception and not necessarily to its directly aural properties; this at any rate would explain why he regarded these principles as applicable equally on all levels of musical structure. But if this theoretical foundation is as uncertain as would appear to be the case, are not the deductions made from it equally suspect? In short, what point can there be in deriving the immediately obvious aspect of the music - our aural and aesthetic experience of it - from complex formal or psychological structures whose reality is at best incapable of demonstration and at worst non-existent?

Criticisms of this sort have repeatedly been levelled, notably by Wittgenstein, against the theories on which the practice of psychoanalysis is based. Freud originally trained as a neurologist, and though his mature theories were no longer couched in literally psychological terms his concepts of 'the libido', 'the id' and so forth constantly give the impression that these might be real entities, perhaps with real locations, in the same sense as 'the liver', 'the pancreas' and so on.[6] In other words Freud analyzed abnormalities of behaviour on the model of physical ailments.

Consequently when he diagnosed a mental illness, he saw himself as discovering the causes of the patient's abnormal behaviour - causes which were in the first instance psychological but which Freud believed to be ultimately a matter of traumatic events in the patient's early life. Just as in other branches of medicine, so in psychoanalysis a diagnosis might be expected to lead to efficacious treatment only if it were factually correct: if for example the psychoanalyst's reconstruction of the original trauma was historically accurate, in essentials at least. Now Wittgenstein's argument[7] was that psychoanalysis does not reveal the causes of a neurosis, whether these causes be defined in terms of the patient's history or in terms of hypothetical processes in his unconscious mind. Wittgenstein questioned the relevance of the first and the existence of the second. Instead he suggested that psychoanalysis should not be regarded as concerned with causes at all, but with reasons. What mattered (Wittgenstein said) was simply that the patient accepted the psychoanalyst's reconstruction of the trauma as explaining his behaviour. The value of such acceptance on the patient's part was that it allowed him to come to terms with himself; the analysis worked because it altered the way in which the patient saw himself. Consequently, Wittgenstein concluded, judgement as to the the correctness or otherwise of a psychoanalytical explanation was not a matter of theoretical validity but a pragmatic one; the analysis that produced the right results was the right analysis.

In the rest of this chapter I shall try to show that Wittgenstein's critique is as applicable to musical analysis as it is to psychoanalysis; for example, it shows us how to resolve the contradiction raised in our discussion of motivic analysis. If we value an analyst's arguments, but not because we believe in the causal theory in terms of which they are expressed, then we must do so because in some way his arguments allow us to account satisfactorily for the music as we experience it. The purpose of analytical argument will thus not be so much to derive strict deductions from undeniable premises, as to persuade the listener or reader to 'hear' or 'see' the music in a certain way. For most analysis is best understood as something more than unsupported assertion about aural experience, but less than rigorous deduction from musical scores. It is more profitable to regard it as informal argument whose aim is not certainty but belief.

Analytical image and analytical listening

Both psychoanalysis and musical analysis involve imagination in the sense that an image is constructed. In psychoanalysis the patient's subjective feelings are externalized: the account of the patient's past built up by the analyst renders these feelings, so to speak, negotiable - the patient comes to terms with them because he is able to 'see' his neurosis from the outside. In the same way musical analysis renders music negotiable because the listener's experience is in some way externalized. To listen analytically, then, is not only to listen but to imagine: when as sometimes happens one begins by listening to a piece casually but after a minute or two finds oneself beginning to analyze it, a definite change has come over one's listening. Questions come to mind, and these questions are fashioned in terms of imagery of some kind: one may for example 'see' a particularly intense chromatic passage as a sort of knot whose strands lead - well, where?

and how? and so the analysis begins.

Analysis is however more than simply listening with imagination; all sorts of images (visual, tactile, kinaesthetic) commonly accompany the experience of music under ordinary concert hall conditions. For instance, if one listens to Ligeti's <u>Atmosphères</u> one may well experience the music in terms of shards of colour, swirling clouds, towering blocks of sound that come closer or retreat into the distance. But such images are unstable and evanescent. By contrast if one listens to the music with a certain degree of analytical attention, then the same visual and spatial imagery may appear (for it is difficult to 'hear' <u>Atmosphères</u> in terms of anything more precise) but it will be more stable and enduring, the spatial coordinates for example corresponding more consistently with the objective tessitura of the perceived sounds. Thus one will 'see' the music as an extended body of sound moving in a stable and continuous space in which it describes recognizable patterns, or which it fills densely or diffusely; not unlike the kind of graphic representation of sound adopted in such early electronic scores as Stockhausen's <u>Studie II</u>.

Because this analytically perceived space has a more or less rational topography, and a more or less consistent reference to the perceived sound, it can to some degree function as an externalized model of the music. For example, the listener may be able to 'stand back' from his immediate aural experience by virtue of recognizing a certain pattern in his spatial image as repeating or transforming some earlier event in the music. The spatial image not only renders relationships of this sort clearly 'visible', but also provides a medium within which immediate connections between temporally removed events can be seen – 'immediate' in the sense of bypassing the listener's experience as a temporally embedded process. Analytical listening, then, involves perceiving the music in terms of a coherent structure independent of the listener, and spatial imagination of this sort must therefore constitute the most rudimentary type of musical analysis. Indeed it often plays an important role in the early stages of the analytical process. If for example one wishes to analyze <u>The Rite of Spring</u> the natural thing to do is to listen to the music several times with the score. This particular score is so awkward to read with all its transposing instruments that at first one tends to look at it rather than read it, treating it as one treats the score of <u>Studie II</u>: that is to say, by associating the sound of a passage with its appearance on the page rather than with the particular intervallic or rhythmic structures the score reveals when read properly. But even looking at the score like this is a form of analysis in that it renders the musical sound more negotiable than is otherwise the case. For example a phrase or a sonority will remind me of something that came earlier: and I flick the pages back, trying to find where it was by means of my memory of what it looked like on the printed page. Or the very look of the page may bring to my notice the repetition or similarity of a texture that I had never observed as such when listening to the music in the ordinary way. So at this stage of the analysis I have learnt to use the score as a kind of physical token of the music. It would be a distinct setback if for some reason I had to change over to another edition of the score in which everything appeared in different positions on the page. Only as my familiarity with the music increases will this dependence on the score as a physical object diminish and be replaced by more flexible and abstract images of musical sound - formal taxonomies, melodic or harmonic evolutions and the like.

Spatial listening of this sort modifies and externalizes the normal experience of music primarily by associating it more closely with the objective properties of the musical stimulus. To 'see' Atmosphères in terms of more or less autonomous dimensions of tessitura, density and so forth is in some degree to become detached from it; that is to say, the judgements involved are more or less independent of aesthetic evaluation. Two listeners who were at loggerheads as regards its musical value might nevertheless agree on a description of the sound in terms of such basic categories as these. Now there are applications in musicological research which call for a more or less objective type of listening that bypasses aesthetic judgement in this manner. A good example is the Cantometrics project. As Alan Lomax describes it, "the cantometric system ... was not set up to describe musical ideolects or dialects or any one musical statement, but to point to differences in style at the regional and areal levels".[8] In other words, the analytical focus is away from the individual musical context, and towards generalizations of a statistical nature. These generalizations are made on the basis of trained listeners' informal ratings of folk songs in terms of a number of predefined stylistic categories. Although informal, these ratings are apparently quite reliable as between one listener and another; with experience, writes Lomax, any student should "fall into a listening pattern which is similar to our own".[9] Now though this listening pattern involves setting up a relatively objective image of the music, there are important aspects in which it is quite dissimilar from 'musical analysis' as the term is generally understood in the context of Western art music. The kind of Schenkerian listening described by Salzer, for instance, is directed at the individual musical context and is predicated on aesthetic reaction: in both ways it is unlike the kind of listening Lomax describes. In fact it can be argued that the purpose of Schenkerian analysis is precisely to define musical contexts, and to do so in terms of the particular relation that holds in that context between the objective properties of the musical sound - what Lomax quantifies - and the aesthetic response to them.

Take the example of repetition. The word may refer either to the objective properties of musical sound or to an aesthetic judgement about musical form; most often however, as is the case with many analytical terms, the word is used to say something about both. Now the relationship between these two aspects is clearly not a direct one, but one that varies with context. It is a common observation that musical forms which on paper appear almost ludicrously short-winded and repetitive may in practice be experienced in terms of a larger, more continuous evolution: I have found children for example to be amazed to discover how little actual music and how much literal repetition there is in the vocal and choral number in the first scene of Purcell's Dido and Aeneas, "Fear no danger to ensue"; they had heard it as continuously evolving sound. And even where repetitions are so small-scale that they cannot possibly be overlooked - for example, the obsessive flattened sixth towards the end of the Pilgrims' March from Berlioz' Harold in Italy - what is experienced is far from being a direct analogue of the objective structure (in the Pilgrims' March the effect is of a tension that at first rises only to dissipate as no resolution is forthcoming, so that the movement is left, so to speak, hanging in the air). To analyze a repetition therefore is not simply to uncover an objective structure, in the manner of Lomax, but to make a connection between the objective structure and the experienced effect - a connection that can only be established in terms of the particular musical context. For example, Carl Schachter's Schenkerian analysis of Schubert's <u>Moment Musical</u> Op. 94/1 attempts to show how what is in objective terms the literal repetition of a section is actually experienced as an ongoing linear evolution - so that the linear reduction of the repeated section is different the second time it appears from the first.[11]

These examples show how far Schenkerian analysis is from being a direct transcription of the objective properties of the musical sound, regardless of context - as is the Cantometric style of listening. Because it involves contextual judgement in this way, the relationship between the different levels of a Schenker analysis is not an exclusively formal one and it is hard to see therefore how it could be expressed in rigorous, axiomatic terms without losing precisely that sensitive adjustment to the individual context that distinguishes a good Schenker analysis from a bad, or even absurd, one. As I remarked in the case of motivic analysis, musical textures are normally so rich that any number of linear reductions are possible if the only requirement is a conjunct scalar fall; practically all tonal music with any amount of figuration can be thus shown to be made up of endless ribbons of scales. The more abstract techniques of musical analysis, such as Allen Forte's applications of set theory, are even more powerful devices than conventional Schenkerian analysis for representing any musical function as specifically related to virtually any other. The substance of the analytical argument therefore lies not so much in the formal demonstration of relatedness - it almost goes without saying that such a demonstration can be made - as in the sensitivity and imagination which are exercised in deciding what to relate to what. Despite the deductive appearance both of Schenkerian and of more formalized analyses, then, it is in the first instance informal criteria that govern the choices made by the analyst; and it is informal criteria by which most musical analyses are in practice assessed, too.

The weakness of set-theoretical analysis, and to a lesser degree of the motivic method of analysis we discussed earlier, is that in neither case do the arguments involved lend themselves very easily to such informal assessment. Particularly in the case of set theory, the reader has more or less to accept or reject the analysis as a package, depending upon the theoretical opinions which he begins with rather than the specific insights that he ends up with. By contrast, the particular strength of Schenker analysis lies in its series of practical (rather than theoretical) demonstrations, which is what the various levels of a Schenker analysis really are. A Schenker analysis can virtually dispense with words, and yet remain a genuine argument, not because there is anything uniquely musical about its basic principles but because these levels can actually be <u>read</u> as music by the reader: read, that is, in the sense of being 'heard' as music and therefore allowing of the immediate verification or refutation of any analytical assertion. Whereas in a set-theoretical analysis any specific demonstration must be done 'blind' through the medium of numerical computation, the argument of a Schenker analysis is (so to speak) aurally translucent at all times. If, to take the simplest possible example, the reader sees the following linear reduction (Ex. 4.4) he does not have to

Ex. 4.4: Brahms, Intermezzo Op. 119/1

figure it out or reconstruct its logic: he merely needs to read it as music, 'hearing' the asserted fall from the F# to the E and asking himself: is that what I hear? is it what I want to hear?

At first sight these are rather different questions. Analysts have on various occasions argued in favour of each being considered the proper topic of analysis. Rosen, for example, argues that the validity of an analysis is a matter of what, as a matter of fact, we do hear: "when there is a correspondence between the detail and the structure [he says], merely to uncover it in the score is insufficient: we must be able to claim that it has always been heard, without being put into words perhaps, but with an effect upon our experience of the musical work".[11] On the other hand, Cone suggests that the point of analysis is to modify what we hear: "the greatest analysts (like Schenker at his best) are those with the keenest ears: their insights reveal how a piece of music should be heard".[12] But probably the distinction between these two positions is more apparent than real. Reactions such as 'yes, that must be how it is' run the two together, and in a sense to draw attention to any aspect of experience is inevitably to modify it; though by definition this cannot be demonstrated, and indeed when a listener has once noticed a certain analytical connection he may find himself unable to believe that he was ever wholly unaware of it. In each case however what is important is the same, namely that an immediate empirical judgement is involved. To analyze, or to read an analysis, is to experiment upon oneself: it is essentially a process of induction rather than deduction, and it is on the results of such empirical tests that the validity of any particular line of argument will be accepted or rejected by the reader. A Schenker analysis is in effect a carefully graded series of such practical tests, the intention of which is to persuade the reader to 'hear' the music in a certain way on the evidence of his own aural imagination. For this reason it is virtually impossible to read a Schenker analysis properly if some other music is within earshot: it is easy enough to <u>see</u> the asserted connections under such circumstances, but it is hardly possible for the reader to come to any conclusions about them unless he can <u>hear</u> them too. And this can be as true on the large scale of, for example, Schenker's analysis of the <u>Eroica</u> Symphony as it is on that of the Brahms example I quoted; large-scale connections of this sort may have no immediate correlate in the listener's experience when the music is heard in the concert hall, but when they are 'heard' in this way by the analyst or composer they can be made the object of an immediate aural judgement.

Properly speaking, then, an analysis is a particular

process of imaginative hearing; the graphic, numerical, or tabular representation that is published is not itself that analysis but merely its vehicle - one might indeed call it a kind of score. And as in the case of the performance score, so in the case of the analytical 'score' the categories employed are often broad and imprecise in the abstract, acquiring a more specific denotation only in a given musical context; only, that is, by virtue of a perceptual judgement by the listener. A conventional formal tabulation of something like Strauss' <u>Ein Heldenleben</u>, for example, means very little in the abtract; categories like 'first subject', 'transition' and 'coda' say virtually nothing about the particular properties of these sections and not much about the relations between them either. On the other hand, if one actually listens to <u>Ein Heldenleben</u> in terms of sonata form (as the clear division of the music into exposition, development and recapitulation suggests one should) then many issues arise that demand quite specific decisions: is the spiky section in a Phrygian G minor after rehearsal number 13 a second subject, or is it better thought of as enclosed within the initial E^b major block? In which case should the two extended sections in G^b major (after numbers 32 and 35) be thought of as the second tonal group and if so why is it still in G^b in the recapitulation (after 91)? And what are we to make of the two codas (if that is what they are), each of which begins with the parallel fifths figure from the G minor section? Why does Strauss have the break at the beginning of the first 'coda' (after number 84), given that the medley of quotations is not yet finished and the recapitulation of the second subject (if that is what it was) is still to come? Or is it hopeless to account for such things except in terms of the traditional programmatic associations, and if so should on think less of the piece because of this? In this way the terminology of conventional formal analysis, although it is loose in itself and rather poorly adapted to Strauss' music anyhow, poses quite specific problems in specific contexts: it leads the reader to ask questions of himself the answers to which involve new judgements about his experience of the music - or perhaps it would be more correct to say, involve new experiences of the music.[13]

It is then rarely correct to judge an analysis purely on the basis of the analytical image as such. Thus it is not to the point that an anaytical representation should contain everything that matters aesthetically about the piece; indeed it is rarely possible, because often what matters to the listener is overwhelmingly the details and an analysis that included all the details would not, after all, be an analysis. A better criterion of the adequacy of an analysis than what it includes is therefore what it omits, while still leaving an image that is intelligible as a vehicle for 'hearing' the music; Schenker's reduction of the Haydn E^b Sonata in <u>Five Graphic Analyses</u>, for instance, is an exercise in omission in which extended circularities of tonal or linear progression are identified and 'bracketed out'. The essential linear skeleton that remains when such elaboratory circuits have been excised is, of course, more or less meaningless in itself; that is, it is without individuality or aesthetic value. Indeed the middlegrounds of Schenkerian analyses are frequently unintelligible considered as possible pieces in their own right; certainly it would be hard to remember in detail how Mitchell's linear reduction of the <u>Tristan Prelude</u>

goes, except by reference to Wagner's music. But this only shows how irrelevant it is to judge, or in general to make substantial deductions of any kind from, analytical images as such: for if these images are merely the visible traces of the analytical listening, then it is in that listening itself that sensible criteria of analytical adequacy will be found.

Criteria of analytical adequacy

I pointed out in Chapter One that analysts routinely describe musical form as something much more complex than listeners ordinarily perceive. And in any case the distinction between form and content in music is always a troublesome one, unless it is made simply in terms of what a composer does; as with proportion, the way form is perceived depends very much on the content, and it could be argued that it is only when the two do not fit together satisfactorily (as in Tchaikowsky's Fourth Symphony, for example) that the listener becomes aware of form as such. In that case why are analysts so taken up with large-scale form, whether in the sense of conventional formal taxonomies, or in the sense of the large-scale unity and directedness discovered by Schenkerian analysis? Why do they spend so much time talking about things that have little or no effect upon the listener's experience of the music? The answer, I think, is that form (in this sense) is not so much the topic of analysis as the means by which analysis of details is done. Details are, after all, aesthetically crucial in music (as in most other arts); it is probably a simple descriptive fact that it is primarily the musical details that please the ear, excite feeling, and lodge in the memory. Schoenberg himself, we are told, had to look hard at

Schenker's graph of the _Eroica_ Symphony before discovering his favourite passages in the tiny notes of the foreground. The story of course makes Schenker's graph appear ridiculous. But Schenker graphs are not intended to be looked at, however hard; they are intended to be read, and to read them is to gain a perception of musical details that is in certain ways quite distinct from that of ordinary listening.

This can be conveniently illustrated by considering in more detail the example mentioned at the end of Chapter One: the _Tristan Prelude_. Listening to it in the normal way, one is aware of its form as a tensional arch that builds up slowly in waves, until a climax is reached at which the music suddenly collapses to reveal a variant of the opening. But one's attention is less engaged by any large-scale formal articulation than by the immediate continuity of the musical growth: the smooth harmonic unfolding, the almost imperceptible development of thematic motives one from another. Afterwards, when one thinks back to the music, what is retained is a generic sense of this unhurried but compelling evolution, coupled with aural memories of details and moments – the first entry of the strings, perhaps, the cathartic #4-3 apoggiaturas, or the modulation (if it can be so called) from the dominant of A to that of C at bar 71. But in terms of its specific evolution the music has become fragmented in the memory: it is difficult to relate these moments to each other, and even perhaps to remember in what order some of them came. Such familiarity can be gained simply by repeated listening: a stage is reached at which one knows what order things come in much as a child knows its alphabet – by 'rehearsing' it until a particular letter is located. An analysis like Mitchell's, however, relates different musical events directly to each other: instead of 'rehearsing' the music as it comes, the analysis makes it easy to 'see' the music as a single spatial extension which can be traversed backwards or forwards: the eye travels up and down the graph too, 'seeing' the music now from a distance and now in terms of foreground detail. I may have a distinct aural memory of two events but cannot think how the music got from one to the other - for example, from the B-area at bar 73 to the B^b-area at bar 81; the middleground of Mitchell's graph makes it easy for me to 'see' them in relation to each other. (Given that the Prelude is in A minor, the B chord becomes part of a V-minor arpeggiation that rises to VI; the B^b, as ^bII, is seen either as an immediate neighbour to this VI on the cycle of fifths, or alternatively as a kind of acoustic underpinning of it: Ex. 4.5.) Or again, Mitchell clarifies the first seventeen

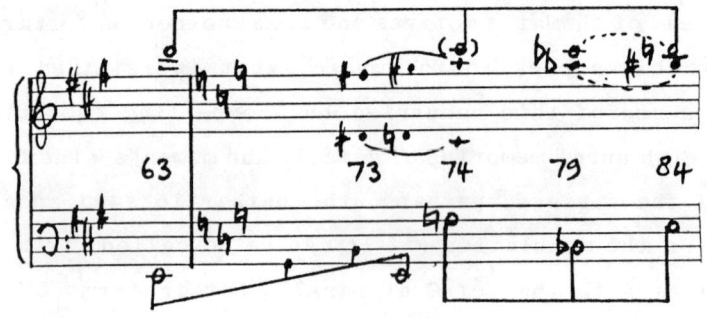

Ex. 4.5: Tristan Prelude, bars 73 - 81

bars as being enclosed within an A that rises through two octaves before rising further to D and falling back to A at the end of the Prelude.

Do I hear the music like this? In a sense the question is unintelligible. I hear what Wagner wrote, not a background or even a middleground formation. What is however clear is that I can easily imagine the music like this; I can easily follow Mitchell's graph as I listen to the music (just as I can follow Wagner's score), and I can easily 'hear' the music as I read through Mitchell's graph; even when I am reading it from top to bottom. That Mitchell's graph renders the music 'negotiable' in a way in which it is otherwise not, then, is a matter of descriptive fact; theoretical issues about <u>why</u> this should be, while possibly interesting, are largely irrelevent from the analytical point of view. Thus Mitchell's analysis shows the Prelude as essentially diatonic, its chromatic elements being merely interpolated between formal pillars or registral lines that are themselves diatonic; but it is at least doubtful how far this is a valid basis for historical or psychological deductions. What is not however in doubt is the fact that the piece is conveniently 'seen' this way. So if Mitchell's graph 'explains' the chromatic details in terms of a diatonic framework, this is explanation in the sense of a detailed and immediately intelligible representation, rather than in the sense of strict derivation from theoretically established causes.

An important criterion of analytical adequacy, then, is that it makes it possible to imagine the music clearly and in detail; that is, to imagine (or to hear imaginatively) what is otherwise merely heard. Thus the discovery of new information is only a tangential function of analysis; the intention is not usually to discover things inaudible to the naked ear, so to speak, in the sense in which a microbiologist discovers otherwise imperceptible organisms by means of a microscope. A better analogy is the bird-watcher who sees many more birds than the average person, simply because he looks harder and in the right places; he looks with imagination and understanding where others look casually. In this sense almost the most important test of an analysis is whether it allows the music to be described in detail; and conversely to have described the music in detail, even if only in ordinary language, is in an important sense to have analyzed it. To say this is of course to set aside the distinction made by Cone and Keller between describing and analyzing (p. 124 above). But then description never is merely descriptive; where two analysts disagree in the formal or thematic interpretation of a piece of music, they are quite likely not to agree even on a straight technical description of the facts, which shows how any such description already involves theorization and the exercising of taste. Again, Alan Walker attacks old-fashioned descriptive analysis on the grounds that "you do not solve problems by describing them".[14] But it is everyday experience that this is just how many problems are solved; indeed without such careful description it is usually difficult to be sure what the problem is in the first place, or in fact whether there really is one at all. So in analyzing music: reading the score several times, describing the music in detail, perhaps parsing the more complex chords – these things are usually more productive than launching immediately into a complex motivic analysis. The tendency, in America at least, to make sophisticated motivic analyses of what can be read as simply chordal progressions derives from trying to draw too distinct a line between describing and analyzing; and from thinking that analysis can only have content if it involves deriving the music from explicit theoretical principles of some kind.

This again has an analogy in Wittgenstein's critique of psychoanalysis. He pointed out that the real value of Freud's work lay in his detailed descriptions of clinical cases. To do this Freud required some kind of theoretical framework. He isolated symptons, or grouped certain kinds of behaviour together, by ascribing them to hypothetical causes of a neurological or quasi-neurological nature. But the value of the theory (Wittgenstein suggested) lay in the detailed description it made possible, and not the other way round.[15] So, it can be argued, in music. As analysts we derive musical experience from obscure psychological entities or from formal structures which nobody perceives; we mix terms referring to what performers do with others that relate to the effect made upon the listener; we use metaphors (like 'cadence') and other terms (like 'tonic') which it is almost impossible to define except ostensively - thus children are taught what a tonic is by being played some music and then told: *this* is what a tonic is. The terminology we use, in other words, is not genuinely analytical in the sense of distinguishing cause from effect. When we say that a listener perceives something - a final tonic, say - we also mean to say that he perceives it in a certain way, so that what we are essentially doing is describing a plenum of musical behaviour and experience rather than extrapolating such objectively functioning components of this plenum as research into the psychology of intonation, for instance, might uncover.[16] Rather than making sense in terms of theoretical generalization from particular instances, then, our ordinary analytical vocabulary (and this includes such practically useful, if theoretically obscure, terms as the musical 'idea') is better adapted for the detailed description of specific musical contexts; provided that the description is not only made but also understood in an informal and musically sensitive way.[17]

The conventional vocabulary for music, then, describes musical phenomena largely by a kind of metaphorical explanation, in which they are derived from one hypothetical cause or another - harmonic or motivic prototypes, unconscious psychological processes, supposedly biological principles and so forth. Though capable of accounting for the music in detail, descriptions of this sort are not necessarily neutral. (Again this applies to psychiatry too: the anti-psychiatry movement sees the treatment of such conditions as schizophrenia as disastrously distorted by the medical metaphor into which psychiatry is locked.) Even an ordinary-language description of music distorts the ordinary experience of it, not only because the words are vague where the music is precise (and vice versa, too) but also because merely to attempt such a close description is to start listening in a new and more self-conscious manner. Any description of music, whether verbal or graphic, is likely to exaggerate characteristics and heighten contrasts. The graphs of music 'seen' in terms of one parameter or another, and which are widely used in American pedagogical texts, do not simply represent the listener's experience of music (or even an aspect of it) in a neutral, descriptive manner. Rather they present familiar phenomena out of context, seen from unfamiliar angles like the 'trick photographs' popular in children's comics. They make structures stand out in much the same way as a microscope slide that is stained in order to reveal formations otherwise hard to pick out. That indeed is why they are interesting. And again, the ability of an analysis like Mitchell's to present musical details as related directly to each other is inseparable from a distortion of the musical effect: tonal areas for example that are experienced as remote or provisional being 'seen' as connected and secure. The music appears as it were written in stone.

In this way discrepancies between musical experience and analytical accounts arise not so much through the inadequacy of analytical terminology as because such accounts relate to what I have several times called the back of the musical fabric. To 'hear' the musical fabric from behind, rather then simply hearing it from the front, is to perceive the actual music as an instance of what is possible; it creates a kind of penumbra of imaginary pieces round the real one. Indeed the 'reality' of the music is abolished, to the extent that it can be 'heard' this way or that, at will. Even at quite an elementary level analyzing music has this creative aspect; that is why it has become one of the principle techniques used in the teaching of composition (and regarded as a means of teaching composition, there is no difficulty in saying that some music is better for analyzing than other music - just as some music is better for instrumental teaching than other music). At a more sublime level, the link between analysis and composition can at times be very strong, particularly when the analysis involved is of as rather speculative nature. In a sense analysis lends itself better to extreme speculation than does composition, simply because the music is already secure: one can analyze in a partial and subjective manner, and possibly with interesting results, whereas to compose in such a way courts disaster. The total-serial composers of the post-war generation clearly derived a great deal of inspiration from an analytical approach to Schoenberg's and Webern's music that was not only wildly speculative but, in some respects, downright unmusical.

To attempt to set up invariant criteria of analytical adequacy is, then, a difficult task and perhaps a pointless one. There are too many contradictions. Generally some kind of sensitivity and truth to experience is such a criterion: one says, that's exactly how it is. On the other hand, the total-serial approach just mentioned was musically insensitive to the point of brutality, and yet served an aesthetic purpose. As a second instance, some kind of aesthetic response to the piece is by and large a prerequisite for decent analysis; without it, half the equation of musical structure and response is lacking, and the exercise degenerates into mechanical deduction from symbols. On the other hand, analysis can now and then create an aesthetic response where there was none before, or add a dimension to it that was otherwise lacking - as in the depth Schoenberg's Five Orchestral Pieces acquire through analysis, or the sense of sleepwalking intuition gained by analyzing Bartok's Second Quartet; in such cases it is difficult to draw a line between technical analysis and the aesthetic perception of form discussed in Chapter One. And clearly if such a line is to be drawn at all it cannot be done in the abstract, but only in relation to the individual piece.

Nor is it sensible to make definite judgements about the adequacy of one analytical method as against another in the abstract. Analytical theories are not valid or invalid in the sense that scientific theories are, or aesthetic theories attempt to be. It is not as if any method can be founded directly on objective principles, or as if an analytical theory could be invalidated by counter-instances;[18] it is not as if adoption of one technique meant the automatic rejection of all others. Again it is a question of the particular piece;

certain methods work well for certain styles, and for certain styles or certain pieces nothing seems to work. Just as important, it is a question of who the analysis is done for. Again this is unlike science: the explanation of the internal combustion engine, for example, is the same whether it is intended for schoolchildren or expert mechanics; it is just that in the first case it is necessary to simplify the way it is put and the detail involved. By contrast, complex ways of analyzing music cannot really be simplified, because they involve complex ways of 'hearing' the music. For an audience of schoolchildren it would be necessary to do a simple analysis, not a simplified version of the complex analysis. And finally, and again unlike scientific research which is commonly regarded as self-justifying, the adequacy of an analysis depends on the purpose for which it is wanted. Yet again, invariable criteria are not possible here because different purposes are involved, such as education at whatever level; or as an aid to performance (for example in the judgement of large-scale dynamics and rhythm, or simply in the memorization of music that tends to ramble, like Schubert Impromptus); or as a source of compositional speculation – any of these is a possible reason for analyzing, so that the judgement of the adequacy of an analysis must be essentially a pragmatic, and sometimes even a subjective, matter. However the issue of analytical purpose does at least allow one more or less invariable criterion for bad analysis. This is the analysis that is begun with no sense of purpose simply because the music is there; which is carried out according to some predetermined plan; and which results in some complex tabulation of results whose precise significance nobody can quite figure out.

Analysis and contemporary musical culture

The account of musical analysis I have offered does not merely run counter to some of the existing theory of musical analysis; it also runs counter to analytical practice in some ways. To an outside observer, the musical analyst must appear to operate in a manner not dissimilar to a scientist, a linguist or a historian: that is to say, as a more or less detached research worker whose business is to contribute to the store of existing knowledge. By and large analysis has become incorporated within the knowledge industry; meaning not only that it is done by specialists at universities but also that a professional analyst is expected to publish his results much like any other academic. Both in Europe and America the post-war period has seen the production of a number of scholarly journals devoted to musical analysis, and the format of thse publications generally resembles that of the scientific paper. Individual compositions, or sometimes parts of them, are treated more or less as case-studies in the course of which principles of a more general theoretical nature are deduced and tested; as Babbitt puts it, the aim is to develop "a higher level theory, constructed purely logically from the empirical acts of examination of the individual compositions".[19] The point is not therefore simply to acquaint the reader with a piece, but to conduct a theoretical argument of some nature. Moreover people will frequently read these articles not so much because they have any immediate interest in the piece under discussion but because they are interested in the theoretical conclusions. This is particularly the case when the journals concerned – <u>The Music Forum</u> and <u>Perspectives of New Music</u> in particular – are associated with a particular analytical approach;

they tend therefore to be house journals, in that the emphasis tends to be upon the solidarity of the theoretical approach rather than the diversity of the individual compositions under discussion. To this extent individual pieces are used like carefully designed experiments: not so much as the topic of research as the means by which it is carried out.[20]

In part this official face of contemporary analysis, so to speak, is a misrepresentation of analytical practice. In the first place there is, as my description suggests, a tension within published analysis between the disinterested, deductive style and the committed and even proselitizing intention. Although analyses, like detective stories, purport to start with the evidence and finish with the conclusions, both are in reality written as much backwards as forwards: that is to say, the analyst begins with a certain 'vision' of the piece which he then sets about detailing and justifying by means of whatever evidence may be available. That, after all, is why he chooses to analyze that particular piece in the first place. But more important than this tension within published analysis - which is in any case not uncharacteristic of scientific research too - is the extent to which published analysis is untypical of the bulk of actual analytical practice. For most analysis is done orally or privately and never published at all. Thus the published format favours originality of interpretation and comprehensiveness of treatment; it involves taking an analysis to a much higher degree of completion than is usually the case in an educational context. It throws all the weight on the conclusions reached, whereas much classroom analysis comes to very little in the way of conclusions. For example in analyzing Liszt's B minor Piano Sonata one might ask: do you hear the opening as a minor-mode elaboration of VI that falls by step onto the fifth of the tonic triad at bar 14? Or do you hear that first B minor chord of the piece as a dissonance in relation to what has come before, in which case when do you begin to hear B minor as a tonic? Questions like this hardly need a definite answer; their purpose is to elicit that kind of large-scale, voluntary 'hearing' - now this way, now that - of which analysis proper consists, and which is more or less a prerequisite for musical compositon. Again, one might ask: what are the chords underlying the two extended chromatic falls in, for instance, Chopin's E minor Prelude? and frequently the answer to questions of this sort is that there is no real answer, for it makes just as good sense to derive what Chopin wrote from a number of chordal prototypes. Indeed there is hardly more point in attempting definite conclusions about how the 'Tristan chord' should be derived. But in neither of these cases is the exercise abortive within an educational context, because the demonstration that there is no particular answer is sufficient to help break down the normal tendency to think in block chords guitar-fashion; sufficient also to illustrate the way in which Romantic composers softened the harmonic rhythms of classical music, melting the walls between one chordal cell and the next so that their harmonic colours intermingled. In ordinary practice, then, the value of an analysis is not coextensive with that of the conclusions reached. And finally, published analysis lays much more stress on theoretical consistency than does common analytical practice. A published Schenkerian analysis is generally not only an analysis but also Schenkerian, in the sense that it either confirms or modifies Schenkerian principles in a coherently argued manner. By contrast unpublished analysis is frequently eclectic and pragmatic, techniques being tried out, altered or improvized entirely on the basis of the particular application. As we've seen, theory of some kind is almost inevitably implicated in analysis, if only because one so often describes musical details by deriving them from something; but in the classroom the emphasis is more on the immediate intelligibility of a description than on the consistency of its theoretical implications. As in history,[21] general theoretical principles are more often than not invoked as a starting point for the discussion of the specific instance, rather than the other way round. In practice, therefore, musical analysis is primarily directed at the individual.

However the scientific bent of musical analysis is not entirely to be explained away in terms of the discrepancy between analytical theory and analytical practice. At the beginning of Chapter One I spoke of the origins of 'functionalist' analysis in a specific early twentieth-century aesthetic stance. Ornamentation, entertainment value and emotional or theatrical effect were all downgraded; in their place an overwhelming emphasis was placed on structural integrity — on the 'purely musical', as both Schoenberg and Schenker put it, rather than the 'extra-musical'. Analytical techniques were therefore sought which would represent music in terms of precise structural relations rather than in terms of purely traditional forms or vague literary associations. And this approach to music in terms of explicit logical relationships received a further impetus after the Second World War, on both sides of the Atlantic. In Europe the generation of composers who emerged in the 1950's attempted to wipe the slate clean, so to speak, by taking music back to first principles: splitting the material of music back into its constituent parameters and rebuilding it into explicitly ordered structures from which all the suspect imponderables of historical style and emotional association had been excised.[22] In America too music was reduced to logical principles, although here the tone of the transformation was more rational and indeed more academic than was the case in Europe; the aesthetic predeliction Babbitt's and Boretz' compositions show for objectivity, precision and complexity was rationalized and justified by reference to the tenets of logical positivism. These, then, were the contexts in which the principal schools of musical analysis current today developed; and each was an aesthetically-charged context. Indeed each of the principal anaytical methods has remained more or less closely associated with a particular repertoire for which it functions as a kind of apologia; analytical knowledge is thus embedded in musical practice.

So musical analysis is not without its contradictions. Its style is largely scientific; but it is so for aesthetic as much as scientific reasons. Each analytical method claims, or at least implies, a universal application because derived from first principles; but the very programme of deriving music from first principles, and so explaining it in theoretical terms, betrays a specific aesthetic stance and thus precludes universal application. If, therefore, analytical explanation is not detached from musical culture (in the way that scientific explanation aims to be), then its development cannot be purely technical. New analytical methods arise not so much from technical advances as from changing aesthetic interests. If some of the theorizing about music current in the earlier part of this century no longer seems as convincing or important as it once did, this is not because we know more about music than was the case then, but because our musical values are no longer quite the same.

Notes

1: That of Oedipus is published: Stravinsky's Oedipus as 20th-Century Hero.

2: For an illustration see Harvey, The Music of Stockhausen, p. 70.

3: Schoenberg's concept of the unity of musical time and space (see e.g. Rufer, Composition with Twelve Notes, p. 49) is given a specifically Freudian interpretation by Keller in The Chamber Music, p. 116. Sources for many of my statements in this paragraph will be found in Keller's article.

4: Keller, The Chamber Music, p. 92.

5: Cf. Nordmark's criticisms of Reti, New Theories of Form and the problem of Thematic Identities.

6: See MacIntyre, The Unconscious: a Conceptual Analysis, p. 23.

7: See Scruton, Aesthetics of Architecture, p. 147.

8: Lomax, Folk Song Style and Culture, p. 31.

9: Ibid, p. 36.

10: In Yeston, Readings in Schenker Analysis, p. 183. For a detailed discussion of the analytical significance of repetition see Meyer, Explaining Music, p. 44 ff.

11: The Classical Style, p. 141.

12: Analysis Today, p. 36.

13: Similarly apparently loose descriptions – this is a noble piece – can have quite a precise content when interpreted as 'you should hear this piece as noble'. What is less appropriate is to treat 'noble' as a category of significance in itself, for example by tabulating 'noble' pieces so as to extrapolate their invariant properties, in the manner of Deryck Cooke: considered in the abstract the term is really too vague for such deductions to be worthwhile. The same arguably applies to tabulations of form, tensional morphology and so forth.

14: <u>A Study in Musical Analysis</u>, p. 23.

15: MacIntyre, <u>The Unconscious: a Conceptual Analysis</u>, p. 72.

16: Because the distinction conventional terminology makes between what is perceived and how it is perceived is not a genuinely functional one, attempts to derive the history of musical artefacts from the historical development of musical listening invariably become circular. Lissa's <u>On the Evolution of Musical Perception</u>, for instance, reads much like any other history of music, except that the usual nouns have been replaced by verbs; the distinction between the musical structures that are perceived, and the particular ways in which they are perceived, cannot be sustained.

17: This invention of unverifiable psychological and other entities in order to 'derive' musical descriptions from them (motivic derivations, harmonic derivations and so forth) has a parallel in music history. Particularly in the earlier part of the present century, ideal and quite unverifiable 'histories' of primordial music were developed whose value clearly lay in educational presentation: see Allen, <u>Philosophies of Music History</u>, p. 306.

18: Martin, <u>Modes of Explanation in Analytical Discourse</u>, p. 177.

19: <u>The Structure and Function of Music Theory</u>, p. 10-11.

20: Indeed Babbitt has associated composers in this scientific enterprise too: "every musical composition justifiably may be regarded as an experiment, the embodiment of hypotheses as to certain specific conditions of musical coherence" (<u>Twelve Tone Rhythmic Structure and the Electronic Medium</u>, p. 148).

21: Gardiner, <u>The Nature of Historical Explanation</u>, p. 90.

22: Thus, for example, Krenek described the purpose of total serialism as "to set up an impersonal mechanism" in place of an inspiration that had become discredited "because it is not really as innocent as it was supposed to be, but rather conditioned by a tremendous body of recollection, training and experience" (Extents and Limits of Serial Technique, p. 90).

Summary

Chapter One began by describing how the 'functionalist' aesthetic of the early twentieth century composers and analysts resulted in music being seen as the communication of structural intentions. Consequently they regarded musical listening as a high-level mental process in which the musical form is reconstructed by the listener according to compositional categories, or at least categories bearing some functional equivalence to the composer's. Indeed this was widely accepted as an aesthetic criterion for art music (as opposed to entertainment); hence also the emphasis that has been placed on musical form, since to hear music as form means hearing it in terms of explicit relationships of musical structures communicated through, but logically independent of, musical sound. This description, I argued, applies well enough to the type of listening done by students in aural training sessions; they are consciously engaged in identifying musical structures in just this way. But does the same happen in the concert hall? It could, of course, be argued that in ordinary musical listening discriminations of this sort do happen, but unconsciously; consideration of this possibility was postponed to Chapter Three. Certainly the conscious experience of musical form in the concert hall seems to be as much a matter of subjective imagination as of perceiving the music in terms of explicit compositional categories. In fact, I argued, the purely perceptual basis of musical form is much less elaborate than analysts would normally imply - meaning by this, the extent to which changes in the musical structure result in equivalent changes in the listener's experience of it. And it is obvious that musical textures are heard primarily in terms of overall effect rather than of relationships between perceived elements. Could it then not be argued that the experience of music is really nothing more than a matter of psychological reactions to presented stimuli, and therefore that composing music is merely a matter of predetermining the effects these stimuli are to make? To assert this, and thereby wholly reject the 'functionalist' aesthetic, would (I argued) be to go too far; imagination and even reasoning, in the sense of the listener's voluntary decision as to how he will hear music as form, are indeed involved in hearing music. But they are only involved at a fairly rudimentary level, and many of music's most typical characteristics only make sense on the assumption that the listener experiences music at quite an elementary level of consciousness - certainly more elementary than analysts seem to have generally supposed. If confusion is to be avoided, therefore, it is not enough merely to consider the formal properties of musical forms. Rather it is necessary to distinguish the various different ways in which people listen to music for different purposes, some of which are not directly concerned with aesthetic values at all: the complexities of musical form described by analysts may be perceptible (though often they are clearly not), but this does not mean that they are perceived as such in ordinary listening, or even that they make any contribution to the ordinary listener's experience of the music at all. The chapter ended on a question: why then, as analysts, do we account for music in so much more elaborate and conceptual a manner than we experience it as listeners?

In Chapter Two I argued that discrepancies of this sort are typical of the relationship between listening to music and imagining it. Though people without musical training may have an image of clear and vivid musical sound, what they are imagining is not so much actual sound as the general qualities of sounds - as they discover when they try to write down what they are imagining or to pick it out at the piano. Through training, musicians develop the ability to imagine music in much greater detail by coordinating musical sound with imagery that is not in itself aural but rather associates sound with kinaesthetic or symbolic structures. However such images are always incomplete representations of musical sound, and involve what I called its 'deconstruction'; this was illustrated by an account of the process of reading music.

Making music (both in performance and in composition) consists largely of dealing with it in a state that has no direct correlate to the ordinary listener's experience. I compared musical sound to an embroidered fabric: musicians often work, so to speak, on the back of the fabric. Thus the importance of the imagery employed by performers and composers is not that it directly represents what can be heard (and so judged by ear) but precisely that it represents such aspects of musical organization as are not directly audible. And even when composition is done by ear - working out a passage at the piano, say - the composer is not usually listening to the piano as literal sound; instead he is 'hearing' it as a model of the sound he intends. Classical style is so formed that its orchestral textures make sense when heard on the piano, or when reduced to a series of harmonies, or to a single melody: the final effect can be predicted from the reduction, so that even complex textures or large-scale progressions can be designed by ear. Such prediction is much more difficult in twentieth century music. However, I argued, prediction is by no means the sole purpose of the various models of musical sound composers use; serialism for instance represents the audible properties of musical sound only poorly, but the very discrepancy between sound and image seems to be a source of compositional inspiration. Far from being a neutral medium for musical sound, I concluded, the means by which music is imagined constitute one of the main factors in the formation of musical style.

From here the main thread of the argument continued to the theory of musical analysis set out in the final chapter; Chapter Three represented a detour. In it I attempted to dispose of the idea that musical analysis is (or should be) analogous to scientific explanation, in the sense of explaining what is overtly experienced in terms of underlying factors that are themselves hidden. I began by showing that any such explanation of music must either be specifically psychological or else (as in the case of social interpretations of musical meaning, or formalistic analyses) reducible to a psychological formulation. I tried to show the kinds of psychological hypothesis implicit in twentieth century methods of analysis; Schenker and (to a lesser degree) Schoenberg believed musical structures derived more or less directly from natural laws of biology or acoustics, whereas post-war analysts generally assume that a logical distinction can be made between the formal structure of music – which is the province of the analyst proper – and the sonic material in which it is embedded. Hence their attempt to 'delete' the musical listener and instead analyze musical scores in a rigorously deductive manner. The rest of the chapter argued against the attempted identification of analytical and psychological categories on which all such analysis is based, and hence against the analogy between analytical and scientific explanation.

My principal objection was that deductive analyses are based on conventional scores which are not an objective representation of musical data. On the one hand they cannot be related to the physical sound of music except by means of some kind of contextual analysis involving psychological attributions of pitch; but on the other hand they are no more than an approximate guide to the judgements of pitch performers and listeners actually make, so that the deductive analysis of a score probably reveals more about the properties of notation than the particular music in question. A second line of argument was directed at the logical distinction between the formal structure of music and its sonic medium: whereas such a distinction forms a necessary stage in speech perception, I argued, in the case of music it only occurs by virtue of aural training which involves a type of perception quite independent of ordinary musical listening. My final argument returned to the score, showing it to be primarily a representation of 'the piece' as an invariant between one performance and another – an invariance which however is purely aesthetic and hence not reducible to a formal theorem. Compositional design, which is the level at which analysts are principally interested in music, cannot be deduced from a genuinely objective representation of musical sound; analysts, in other words, are rarely if ever engaged in explaining music in a scientific sense.

In Chapter Four I resumed the main thread of the argument that was broken off at the end of Chapter Two, setting out a rationale of analytical practice on the basis of the discussions of musical listening and musical imagination in the first two chapters. My intention in this chapter was not to propose new techniques of analysis but to clarify why analysis is done as it is done, given that analysis which is of intuitively obvious value is often based on theoretical principles that are dubious at best. I began by discussing various types of argument employed in musical analysis, pointing out that deduction from notational categories is a useful technique provided it is seen only as the basis of straightforward formal descriptions, or of statements of historical fact which are in principle capable of verification. However, I argued, most analysts do not restrict themselves in this way; and we generally value analyses because they do allow us to account for our experience of music, even though the formal or psychological theory behind the analysis may sometimes be obscure or even demonstrably false. I compared this apparently paradoxical stuation with psychoanalysis, suggesting that the argument from hypothetical cause to effect of which most musical analysis consists should be seen as Wittgenstein suggested psychoanalysis should be seen - that is, as an explanation in terms of reasons rather than causes. The difference is that whereas a cause is (in principle at least) a matter of verifiable fact, a reason is a matter of belief; I proposed that the majority of analytical argument is best regarded as an attempt to persuade people to 'see' music in a certain way, just as the psychoanalyst persuades his patient to 'see' himself in a certain way.

I pursued this analogy by showing how analyzing music involves creating an image that represents the musical sound as a structure independent of the listener (in the same way as the psychoanalyst's reconstruction of the case history). I showed how this was not simply a matter of strict deduction but involved making contextual judgements about the musical effect. I argued that the strength of Schenker analysis is that it consists of a series of practical demonstrations, in which the listener accepts the analysis only by virtue of self-experimentation in which he asks himself: is that how I hear the music? is that how I want to hear it? Properly speaking it is listening in this imaginative way that constitutes the analysis: the image which prompts it is no more than a vehicle, and is more or less without significance considered as a structure in its own right. In this way, I argued, analytical accounts of large-scale form (which, as we saw, bulk much larger in analysis than in the listener's experience) function primarily as vehicles for the description, location and precise imagination of musical details. Analysis 'explains' music in the sense of describing it in detail, of rendering it negotiable, rather than in the sense of showing it to be a consequence of external causes; and this means that the methodological distinction between 'description' and 'analysis' proposed by some theorists cannot be sustained.

However describing music in detail is, I argued, only one benefit of analysis. To analyze music is to hear it imaginatively; hence accounting for it as it is merges, so to speak, into accounting for it as it is not. Analysis is as much a medium of compositional speculation as of objective explanation. For this reason it is inappropriate to look for invariable criteria of analytical adequacy, or for general reasons for adopting any one analytical technique as against another; such things can only be judged pragmatically, in the light of the particular piece concerned and - no less important - the purposes for which the analysis is being done. For analytical explanation is not like scientific explanation, that is to say deriving directly from the properties of what is to be explained, and so standing outside cultural needs and interpretation. On the contrary, analysis is an integral part of twentieth century musical culture, as is shown by the close association of particular analytical methods with particular repertoires; each method involves a particular aesthetic stance, which it serves to justify. Even the scientific cast of current analysis - the attempt to explain music logically, in terms of first principles - itself derives from the aesthetic context described in Chapter One; so that it would be only natural if the current revival of nineteenth century values in musical composition were to prompt a similar trend in analysis - for instance, a return to close description of the effect music makes on the listener. At the same time, I argued, the scientific facade of published analysis is not representative of the bulk of practical analysis done in educational contexts, which is eclectic and pragmatic, and in which the emphasis is on the value of the analytical process itself rather than necessarily on that of the conclusions reached.

List of sources cited

Abraham, Gerald: A Hundred Years of Music. London 1974

    This Modern Stuff. London 1939

Adorno, Theodor: Introduction to the Sociology of Music. New York 1976

    Philosophy of Modern Music. New York 1973

Allen, Warren Dwight: Philosophies of Music History. New York 1939

Arom, Simha: The Use of Playback Techniques in the Study of Oral Polyphonies. Ethnomusicology, 20 (1976)

Babbitt, Milton: Past and Present Concepts of the Nature and Limits of Music Theory. In Boretz and Cone

    The Structure and Function of Music Theory. In Boretz and Cone

    Twelve-Tone Rhythmic Structure as a Compositional Determinant. In Boretz and Cone

Beament, James: The Biology of Music. Psychology of Music 5/1 (1977)

Benade, Arthur: Fundamentals of Musical Acoustics. Oxford 1976

Blacking, John: How Musical is Man? London 1973

Blom, Eric: An Essay on Listening and Performance. In Bacharach and Pierce (ed), The Musical Companion. London 1973

Boomsliter, P.C. and Creel, W.: Extended Reference: an Unrecognized Dynamic in Melody. Journal of Music Theory 1963

    Research Potentials in the Auditory Characteristics of Violin Tone. Journal of the Acoustical Society of America 51 (1972)

Boretz, Benjamin: Metavariations. Perspectives of New Music, Fall/Winter 1969, Spring/Summer 1970, Fall/Winter 1970, 1971, Fall/Winter 1972, Spring/Summer 1973

Nelson Goodman's Languages of Art. In Boretz and Cone

Boretz, Benjamin and Cone, Edward T.: Perspectives on Contemporary Music Theory. New York 1972

Clifton, Thomas: Music as a Constituted Object. In F. J. Smith (ed), In Search of Musical Method, New York 1976

Collingwood, R.G.: The Principles of Art. Oxford 1938

Cone, Edward T.: Analysis Today. In Lang (ed), Problems of Modern Music. New York 1962

Sound and Syntax: an Introduction to Schoenberg's Harmony. Perspectives of New Music Fall/Winter 1974

Copland, Aaron: Music and Imagination. Cambridge (Massachusetts) 1961

Creel, W., Boomsliter, P.C. and Powers, S.R.: Tone Sensations as Perceptual Forms. Psychological Review 77 (1970)

Davies, John Booth: The Psychology of Music. London 1978

Ehrenzweig, Anton: The Psychoanalysis of Artistic Vision and Hearing: an Introduction to a theory of Unconscious Perception. London 1953

Esper, E.: Max Meyer and the Psychology of Music. Journal of Music Theory 1966

Faltin, Peter: Phänomenologie der Musikalischen form. Wiesbaden 1979

Gardiner, Patrick: The Nature of Historical Explanation. Oxford 1962

Goehr, Alexander: Musical Ideas and Ideas about Music. Birkbeck College, London, 1976

Hampshire, S.: Modern Writers and Other Essays. London 1969

Harrer, G. and Harrer, H.: Music, Emotion and Autonomic Function. In Critchley and Henson (ed), Music and the Brain. London 1977

Harvey, Jonathan: The Music of Stockhausen. London 1975

Harwood, Dane L.: Universals in Music: a Perspective from Cognitive Psychology. Ethnomusicology 20 (1976)

Herriott, Peter: Attributes of Memory. London 1974

Hopkins, Pandora: The Homology of Music and Myth: Views of Levi-Strauss on Musical Structure. Ethnomusicology 21 (1977)

Jakobson, Roman: Six Lectures on Sound and Meaning. Brighton 1978

Jakobson, Roman and Waugh, Linda: The Sound Shape of Language. Brighton 1979

Keller, Hans: The Chamber Music. In Robbins Landon and Mitchell (ed), The Mozart Companion. London 1956

Kolinski, M.: The Structure of Music: Diversification versus Constraint. Ethnomusicology 22 (1978)

Komar, Arthur: Theory of Suspensions. Princeton 1971

Krenek, Ernst: Extents and Limits of Serial Technique. In Lang (ed), Problems of Modern Music. New York 1962

Lannoy, C. de: Detection and Discrimination of Dodecaphonic Series. Interface I (1972)

Lissa, Zofia: On the Evolution of Musical Perception. Journal of Aesthetics and Art Criticism 24 (1965-6)

Liszt, Franz: The Gypsy in Music. London, n.d.

Lomax, Alan: Folk Song Style and Culture. Washington 1968

McDermott, V.: A Conceptual Music Space. Journal of Aesthetics and Art Criticism 30 (1971-2)

MacIntyre, Alastair: The Unconscious: a Conceptual Analysis. London 1958

Martin, Henry: Modes of Explanation in Analytical Discourse. Perpectives of New Music Spring/Summer 1977

Mellers, Wilfred: Stravinsky's Oedipus as 20th Century Hero. In Lang (ed), Stravinsky: a new appraisal of his work. New York 1963

Merleau-Ponty, Maurice: Phenomenology, Language and Sociology: Selected Essays of Maurice Merleau-Ponty. London 1974

Meyer, Leonard B.: Emotion and Meaning in Music. Chicago 1956

Explaining Music. Berkeley 1973

Music, the Arts, and Ideas. Chicago 1967

Mitchell, William J.: The Tristan Prelude: Techniques and Structure. The Music Forum, I (1967)

Nattiez, Jean-Jacques: The Contribution of Musical Semiotics to the Semiotic Discussion in General. In Sebeok (ed), A Perfusion of Signs. Indiana 1977

Neisser, Ulric: Cognitive Psychology. New York 1967

Nordmark, Jan: New Theories of Form and the problem of Thematic Identities. Journal of Music Theory 1960

Nottebohm, G.: Two Beethoven Sketchbooks. London 1979

Perle, George: Serial Composition and Atonality. London 1968

Plomp, R.: Aspects of Tone Sensation. London 1976

Pousseur, Henri: The Question of Order in New Music. In Boretz and Cone

Risset, J.C.: Musical Acoustics, in Carterette and Friedmann (ed), A Handbook of Perception IV: Hearing. New York 1978

Rosen, Charles: The Classical Style. London 1976

Rothgeb, John. Some Uses of Mathematical Concepts in Theories of Music. Journal of Music Theory 1966

Rufer, Josef: Composition with Twelve Notes related only to one another. London 1954

Ryle, Gilbert: The Concept of Mind. Harmondsworth 1976

Samson, Jim: Music in Transition: a study of tonal expansion and atonality 1900-20. London 1977

Sartre, Jean-Paul: The Psychology of the Imagination. London 1972

Schenker, Heinrich: Free Composition. London 1979

    Harmony. Chicago 1954

Schoenberg, Arnold: Fundamentals of Musical Composition. London 1967

    Style and Idea. London 1975

    Theory of Harmony. London 1978

Schutz, Alfred: Fragments on the Phenomenology of Music. In F.J. Smith (ed), In Search of Musical Method. New York 1976

    Making Music Together. In Collected Papers 2. The Hague 1964

Scruton, Roger: Art and Imagination. London 1974

    The Aesthetics of Architecture. London 1979

Seashore, Carl: The Psychology of Music. New York 1938

Seeger, Charles: Studies in Musicology 1935-75. California 1977

Sergeant, D. and Roch, C.: Perceptual Shifts in the Auditory Information Processing of Young Children. Psychology of Music 1/2 (1973)

Sessions, Roger: The Musical Experience. Princeton 1950

Shepherd, John et al, Whose Music? A Sociology of Musical Languages. London 1977

Smith, F. Joseph: The Experiencing of Musical Sound: Prelude to a Phenomenology of Music. New York 1978

Sudnow, David: Ways of the Hand: the Organization of Improvized Conduct. London 1978

Sutton, R.A.: Concept and Treatment in Javanese Gamelan Music, with reference to the Gambang. Asian Music XI (1979)

Szende, Otto: Intervallic Hearing: its Nature and Pedagogy. Budapest 1977

Vygotsy, L.S.: Thought and Language. Cambridge (Massachusetts) 1962

Ward, W. Dixon: Musical Perception, in Tobias (ed), Foundations of Modern Auditory Theory. New York 1970

Weber, Max: The Rational and Social Foundations of Music. Southern Illinois 1958

Yeston, Maury: Readings in Schenker Analysis and Other Approaches. New Haven 1977

Zuckerkandl, Victor: Man the Musician. Princeton 1976

    Sound and Symbol. Princeton 1962